A WORLD BEGINS

Harrison Smith, Inc., 17 E. 49th St.,
New York City

IRINA SKARIATINA TODAY

A WORLD BEGINS

IRINA SKARIÄTINA

(MRS. VICTOR BLAKESLEE)

1932
HARRISON SMITH & ROBERT HAAS
NEW YORK

TO
MY AMERICAN HUSBAND

ILLUSTRATIONS

A WORLD BEGINS

I

THE heavy train jerked, recoiled and then slowly started to move out of the Petrograd Baltic station. Leaning out of the window of the compartment in which I was destined to travel I waved frantically to the small group of friends that had come to see me off, and as their figures began to recede on the platform tears suddenly streamed down my face.

"Good-by, good-by! I'll come back some day, I'll come back!" I cried, leaning out as far as I could, waving both hands, blowing kisses and sobbing aloud. I knew they could not hear me, but in that moment, when I was leaving Russia, perhaps forever, I felt the need of crying out as loud as I could that some day I would surely come back! Starvation, persecution, imprisonment—nothing could compare to the agony of deliberately leaving my own country and deliberately facing exile.

"Here, you!" a man's voice shouted behind me and as I turned around I saw the train conductor glowering at me angrily. "What's the matter with you," he continued, a nasty sneer distorting his features, "do you think you can behave like this on my train? Remember, times have changed and there is no place now for any of your bourgeois sentimentality."

"I am leaving Russia forever," I cried, but he interrupted me, shouting:

"And a good thing too—the quicker we get rid of the bourgeois the better, though I cannot, for the life of me, see why they let you escape. Prison is the best place for all of you!"

I got angry.

"How dare you criticize the actions of your superior officials?" I retorted. "If they have allowed me to leave Russia—there must be a good reason for that, and you have no business to express any opinion whatsoever. And furthermore," I added, a brilliant thought flashing through my mind, "I think you're a counter-revolutionist and at the first station I'll send the Central Executive Committee a telegram complaining of your behavior and saying that you insulted a passenger who is leaving the country legally with the permission of the Soviet."

This unexpected announcement silenced the man, and for a few seconds he stared at me, evidently trying to make out whether I was in earnest or not, while I glared back at him without winking.

"All right, all right!" he finally said, edging away and muttering to himself as he went.

I sank back on the seat, shaking from head to foot, utterly exhausted by all I had been through in the last few weeks. I was still very weak after my long illness and the slightest exertion tired me out completely. Feeling faint and dizzy I closed my eyes while scenes of the past vaguely floated through my mind. The deaths of my father and mother, both victims of the Revolution, —the uncertainty of life when for five years I never knew whether there would ever be a "to-morrow," the constant hunger, the sordid poverty, the never-ending feeling of exhaustion and weakness and finally imprisonment and the absolute certainty of being put to death. And then, mercifully, the illness that saved my life, as stricken with pneumonia I was transferred from my prison cell to the prison hospital where Dr. Golder of the American Relief Administration found me and pleaded with the bolsheviks for my release and the permission to leave the country, saying that anyway I would probably die in exile very soon.

And here I was, still very shaky after prison and my recent illness, sitting in a train that was carrying me to exile, with no other possessions in the whole world than the old worn out clothes I had on, a very small package of food, one change of underwear, the Soviet passport to leave the country and fifty dollars given to me by the American Relief. How utterly wretched it made me to go. Just then I preferred infinitely the unspeakable life and even death in Russia to exile, and what a hard time Dr. Golder had had, trying to obtain my consent to leave. He thought he was acting for the best, but was he right? I doubted that. What did the future hold for me in foreign countries, weak and penniless, for the fifty dollars could not last long. Would I find work abroad, or would my sister in England be able to take care of me even for a short time? These were the thoughts that passed through my mind as I sat in the corner of the compartment while the train went faster and faster, and the wheels sang louder and louder: "You're leaving forever, you're leaving forever, you're leaving forever!"

Suddenly some one touched me gently and opening my eyes I saw the face of a young woman bending over me—a kindly face with great dark eyes full of pity.

"You're dreaming bad dreams," she said softly, "you were moaning in your sleep and I thought I had better wake you up. Wouldn't you like some hot tea?" she continued, placing a cup in my hand and murmuring

№ 10288   Пролетарии всех стран, соединяйтесь!

ЗАГРАНИЧНЫЙ ПАСПОРТ.

Россійская Соціалистическая Федеративная Советская Республика.

Républíque Socialiste Fédérative des Soviets de Russie.

PASSEPORT.

Prolétaires de tous les pays, unissez-vous!

THE OPENING PAGE OF THE PASSPORT

"drink it all, Galoubouschka,* it will do you good."

The kindness of this total stranger and the warmth of the tea made me feel better at once and, dispelling my painful day-dreams, brought me back to real life.

We were eight women in a compartment intended to contain four passengers and I was lucky to have a corner seat with only one neighbor to crush me instead of being sandwiched in between two. The kindly young woman sat opposite me and evidently was the good genius of the party, for she kept up a gentle flow of soothing talk at the same time continuing to pass around tin cups full of weak tea that she had prepared in an old enamel kettle very much chipped and battered. As the talk was about nothing in particular and my fellow passengers rather uninteresting I soon fell asleep. Suddenly a violent dig in my ribs woke me up with a start and sitting up wildly I saw my old enemy, the conductor, glaring at me once more.

"You're in the wrong compartment, citizeness," he roared, "get out of here, quick, or I'll throw you out. . . ."

"I'll send that telegram about you now—see if I don't," I shouted back. But this time my words did not produce the same effect.

"What kind of a telegram can you send, you—a Countess, of all people!" he snarled contemptuously.

* My little dove.

I stood my ground, though somewhat taken aback that he had discovered my title, saying as forcefully as I could: "I'll send one to Zinoviev and one to Sokoloff, and one to Assniss!"

Again the man looked startled, wavered, then finally, spitting loudly and muttering uncomplimentary things about me, stalked out of the compartment, slamming the door behind him. Triumphantly I looked around while my companions stared at me in amazement.

"Oh, so you're a bolshevik?" the kind young woman murmured reproachfully, but another woman who had doggedly maintained an unfriendly attitude towards all of us, suddenly beamed at me approvingly.

"So, you're a bolshevik?" she said too, though in a totally different tone of voice, as much as to say, "welcome, comrade, welcome."

"I'm nothing of the kind," I answered both women indignantly, "but I have a permit to leave the country and shall certainly not allow a conductor to insult me."

Barely were the words out of my mouth when my enemy returned, accompanied by another man and, pointing a dirty finger at me, shouted, "Come along!"

"Where to?" I asked with as much dignity as I could muster. But before I could add another word he grabbed me by the shoulder and, jerking me out of my seat and into the corridor, pushed me into another compartment.

"Now you stay here, you 'Countess of the telegrams,'

and don't let me hear one more squeak from you," he said gleefully, again slamming the door as he went out. I found myself in a compartment with ten people in it instead of eight. The minute I appeared there was a murmur of protest.

"We're ten persons in here already and we don't want another one," they all cried in one breath.

"But that man pushed me in here; I don't want to be with you either," I retorted, annoyed at the unfriendly way they were receiving me.

"Look here," said a determined woman of considerable size, "we don't care who brought you here, but out you go, madam," whereupon she too grabbed me by the shoulders and shoved me into the corridor.

"What are you coming out of there for?" roared the conductor, advancing towards me threateningly. "Didn't I tell you to stay in that compartment?"

"But they don't want me in there," I protested, feeling quite upset that no one seemed to desire my company anywhere.

"Not want you? Well, that doesn't surprise me," he chuckled, apparently much pleased with my unpopularity, "but nevertheless you go right back and stay there."

I tried the door,—it was locked.

"Well," he thundered, "what's the matter now, hurry up."

"I can't," I cried furiously, "they won't let me in."

That argument proved effective for he instantly stopped being angry with me and, transferring his wrath in another direction, started to swear at the ten occupants of the compartment, kicking the door that they were evidently holding with all their ten-fold might and main, pounding it with his fists and yelling the most frightful abuses.

But they would not give in!

"In the name of the Soviet government I order you to open that door," he finally roared, while I stood behind him breathlessly watching the outcome of the tussle.

His last words worked like magic. Immediately the door opened and the next instant I was hurried back again into the compartment where my presence was so ardently undesired.

"Now here you are and here you stay," declared my tormentor decisively, mopping his forehead and breathing hard. "You've caused enough trouble already, and the less you are seen and heard the better," he added menacingly, as he turned to leave.

"And now that you are here, where are you going to sit, pray?" asked a very thin man, with unveiled sarcasm. "Of course we're delighted to have you, but I'm very much afraid that you'll have to stand."

"All right, I'll stand." I sighed wearily, leaning

against the door and closing my eyes. I was beginning to feel faint and dizzy again and did not seem to care what was going to happen next.

"Why, she's ill!" I heard some one exclaim.

"That's right," said another voice.

"Oh, poor little thing," cried a third.

Suddenly the attitude of the ten people changed. Some one lifted me gently and laid me on the seat,— some one put a wet handkerchief on my forehead,— some one chafed my hands. Hurried little whispers buzzed over me.

"Cover her up."

"Give her some water."

"No, some food; she's hungry."

"Don't be stupid, how can she eat, she's dying."

"A doctor, call a doctor! Isn't there one on this train?"

Vaguely I remember more whispers, more frantic little consultations right over my head, more advice, more arguments.

"She'll die."

"No, she won't."

"Yes, she will."

"No, she won't."

"Be quiet, she can hear you."

"Put a pillow under her head."

"No, take that pillow away."

"Put her on her back."

"No, put her on her side!"

Then suddenly the aimless flutterings ceased and a new competent voice and two competent hands took charge of the situation.

"Please move away," said that voice authoritatively. "She'll be all right in a minute. It's the usual weakness after illness. One can see that she has been very ill."

After that a blank—then a new sensation of warmth and comfort, followed by the realization of being stretched out full length, with the luxury of a soft pillow beneath my head and a heavy woolly blanket around me.

"I am dreaming again," I thought, but as I opened my eyes I saw the kindly young woman of the first compartment bending over me. "Why are you here? We are eleven people without you," I whispered anxiously, afraid that she also would be chased away. But she shook her head and smiled as she whispered back.

"No, it's all right—you're with us again in the first compartment, and we're glad to have you, Galoubouschka—go to sleep, go to sleep."

It was so wonderful to be stretched out, to be warm, to have some one watching over me—that before I knew it I was fast asleep.

"Well, if she isn't back again here where she doesn't belong. How did she get here?" a familiar voice broke through my lovely slumbers, while the familiar hand of the conductor clutched my shoulder and gave me the usual shake.

"I don't know how I got here, some one must have brought me here," I answered apologetically. But he wouldn't believe me.

"You're lying, citizeness, and for that I'll see that you get properly punished," he shouted, tugging at me to make me get up and awakening all the other women by the noise he was making.

"See here, comrade," spoke up the bolshevik girl. "I'm getting tired of all your nonsense. Don't you see she is ill? Well, leave her alone and get out of here yourself—hear me? My name is Comrade T. and if you must have an argument we'll have one in the morning, but now leave us alone—good-by." And giving him an energetic slap on the back she actually got rid of the man and at last we were left in peace.

Our heavy train, consisting of freight cars, with the exception of one passenger car in which we were traveling, progressed very slowly, constantly stopping at all the stations so that it took us an endless time to reach the frontier. Here our solitary passenger car was detached from the train, sidetracked and locked for several hours while evidently some formalities were going on. Only the regular bolshevik passengers were allowed to get off before the doors were locked; we the "exiles," nineteen in all, had to sit patiently like prisoners and wait until we were let out.

At last, in the middle of the night, we were awakened by our conductor, who apparently had been left in charge of us, and ordered to dress and get out as fast as we could. Shivering from cold and weariness we obeyed and climbing down the steps of the car found ourselves on a small wind-blown platform, where our commander-in-chief, assisted by ten soldiers, imposingly armed from head to foot, called out our names and made us stand in line as we answered. Satisfied that we were all there he yelled "Forward! March!"—and off we went across a muddy field in the direction of a long and low log-cabin which turned out to be the customs house. Not having any luggage, except my small bundle with the change of underwear and the food, nor anything concealed on my person, I went quite cheerfully, casting pitying glances at those fellow exiles who were carrying bags and large parcels, and wondering what the fate of their possessions would be.

Arrived at the customs, we women were separated from the men and taken into a small room, where female attendants undressed us and, leaving us without a stitch of clothes on, thoroughly searched every single article that we had worn, ripping open the linings, cutting slits in the soles of our shoes to make sure we had not concealed any papers and, for the same reason, breaking up all the bread, potatoes and even cakes of soap that we had brought with us.

After an hour of this steady destructive work the room we were in was in the most perfect mess I have ever seen—just as though a dozen playful puppies had been let loose and had had the time of their lives! To make our discomfort complete the place was horribly damp and cold. I sneezed, then some one behind me sneezed, then a girl next to me, and soon we were all sneezing in chorus. Our chief woman undresser looked at us disapprovingly as she muttered to her assistants:

"Aren't we the delicate ladies, sneezing away in a nice warm room like this?"

And as we went on sneezing she suddenly lost all patience, stamped her foot, cried shrilly "Stop it!" and then, as we did not obey, advanced towards us with her hands on her hips.

"I really cannot stop," the girl next to me plaintively said, "besides I have no handkerchief, it's in the pocket of my coat."

"You've got mine too."

"And mine," "and mine," we all chanted miserably, continuing to sneeze and snuffle.

"Have you ever seen such stupid creatures?" demanded the woman of her handmaidens in an aggrieved voice, "no wonder the government is sending them out of the country—nothing but a lot of fools, what?"

By this time our clothes had been thoroughly searched and wrecked and we were allowed to dress. The slit soles of my boots, that had already been none too solid before this customs house operation, clip-clopped mournfully as I started to leave the room,—the lining of my hat hung over one ear, the hem of my skirt flopped against my ankles.

"You look awfully funny," giggled the only young girl of our small group as she followed me into the other room where our luggage was being examined.

"And how about yourself?" I retorted peevishly, "look at your shoes and your coat and your muff! Why, if any one looks a sight—you do!"

"Ladies, ladies," interpolated the elegant member of our party, who still managed to look smart despite the fact that her clothes had been put through the same devastating process as ours. "Ladies, don't argue, pray."

Suddenly I saw that the ostrich feather on her hat had completely uncurled and that the sole of her left boot was decidedly separated from its main body. For some reason that sight cheered me up considerably and I smiled at the lady quite pleasantly, though perhaps with a touch of superiority—for had I not seen something that she, poor thing, had not yet noticed?

In the hall we met the men, looking quite as bedraggled as our feminine group and ever so much more savage. Apparently they did not see the humorous side of the episode and were taking the whole thing in a very serious and tragic way.

"Isn't it funny?" I began in a whisper to Mr. X. the violinist, who happened to be next to me.

"Funny?" he interrupted indignantly, "I certainly don't see anything funny about it. Why, if you saw what they did to my pants you wouldn't say that was funny either."

Unfortunately that started me off in fits of laughter much to the eminent musician's disgust. Then suddenly I heard my name called out, while at the same time several obliging hands behind me pushed me towards a long table where our luggage was being once more examined. Between two enormous suitcases I perceived my own tiny bundle all undone with its contents spilled about: a few hard boiled eggs, some potatoes and two cakes of soap all smashed to a pulp. My underwear lay in a little heap next to the demolished provisions, also the tiny red velvet bag in which I had brought some Russian soil that I had dug up before leaving and was taking with me into exile. As I came up to the table I saw one of the officials busily sifting my soil through a sieve.

"What are you doing that for?" I inquired anxiously, fearing that he would spill some of the precious stuff. "Do be careful."

"I am trying to find out what you are concealing in

that earth," he answered. "You surely have something mixed up with it, gold or diamonds perhaps—for certainly no one in her right mind would be foolish enough to carry just a handful of plain, ordinary soil."

"But I *am* foolish enough to do it," I cried. "It's just as you say—plain, ordinary Russian soil that I am taking with me abroad. If I die there they'll put it in my grave."

"Sounds like awful nonsense to me," said the man suspiciously. "But I have not found anything concealed in it,—so I suppose you may have it, though perhaps I'd better throw it away."

"Oh, no, no—don't do that," I pleaded, "there's nothing in it, and it really means a great deal to me."

"All right, all right," he answered quite good humoredly, "you may have your 'estate,' citizeness, but see that you have a nice big house built on it." And very pleased with his joke he grinned broadly and actually put the soil back quite carefully into the little velvet bag.

"Hum, what's this?" another official next to him asked, showing me a slip of paper that he had found in my pocket. It was a few lines of poetry, written by one of the medical students of my hospital, that evidently I had been carrying around with me without even remembering that I had it.

"It's poetry," I answered foolishly, which made him quite angry.

"I know poetry when I see it, thank you for nothing, citizeness. But what I want to know is whether it has a hidden meaning or not. It might be in code and then we'll have to decode it. Comrade Simon," he continued, turning to one of the armed soldiers, "arrest that person for a while, until I tell you to release her."

Thunderstruck, horrified, I nearly dropped on the floor as a soldier came up to my side, rifle in hand. To think that I could be such a fool as to carry a slip of meaningless poetry in my pocket at a time like this and be arrested for it! How could I ever prove that it was not a message in code? Visions of being sent back to Russia, under arrest and put in prison again, flashed through my mind. What would Dr. Golder say, after having had all the trouble of getting me out of the country? My fellow passengers stared at me aghast as a group of officials bent over my paper and earnestly began to "decode" it. I was so furious with myself I did not know whether to laugh or cry. Everybody was being detained on my account, angry looks were sent in my direction, angry whispers reached my ears. In the background I could see the triumphant face of our train conductor, evidently rejoicing at my predicament.

"I always knew from the very first that she was no good," I could hear him say, "from the time we started and until this very minute she has been nothing but a nuisance, a perfect nuisance."

Finally, after what seemed to me an eternity,—the officials stopped poring over my paper and straightened themselves up.

"We cannot yet determine whether it means anything or not," one of them announced gravely. "If it did, the citizeness would have to be sent back under arrest,—but as we have not found anything proving her guilt and have a doctor's certificate here, saying that she is truly ill, we shall give her the benefit of the doubt and let her continue her journey. However, we will keep this paper and not allow her to have it back in her possession."

I nearly shouted for joy! They could keep all the poetry in the world as far as I was concerned,—the important thing was—that I was free and would not be sent back to prison.

In a few minutes we were allowed to depart and marched to the frontier surrounded by soldiers and with our conductor leading the procession.

At the border we were met by the foreign officials and taken to their customs house. Our Russian military escort departed and only the conductor remained, keeping a wary eye on all of us and especially on me—his chief antipathy. In a large, warm and clean dining room we were given tea and some decent food, while our papers were being examined by the customs authorities. With the unpleasant journey behind us, and feeling much better for a good meal, we all cheered up considerably and sat around the long table sipping the tea and talking contentedly. In the atmosphere of general relief at having safely crossed the border I was quite forgiven for having delayed everybody with my suspicious poem and even mildly teased in a gentle and kindly way, as though they all wanted to show that they were sorry for having been angry with me and had already forgotten the disgraceful episode.

Presently the foreign official reappeared followed by our conductor, who for some reason smiled in an unpleasantly sinister way as his glance rested on me.

"Well, I'm out of his reach now—he can't do anything to me," I thought consolingly, though his expression made me somewhat uneasy.

"Silence!" cried the official.

We obeyed.

"Nineteen Russian citizens have reached the border and, having examined their passports, I have come to tell you that they are in good order and, therefore, all are allowed to enter our country." Here he paused for a minute, while we smiled congratulatingly at each other. "All but *one!*" he continued ominously, "for that passenger's passport is *not* in good order and that passenger will have to be sent back to Russia. So of the nineteen Russian citizens, eighteen may continue their journey, while one has to return."

"But why; who is it?" we cried in a confused and frightened manner.

"Why? Because the visa on that passport is exactly one day overdue and therefore of no value any longer. The passenger should have crossed the border yesterday."

"But who is it, who?" we persisted frantically.

The man smiled in an exasperatingly deliberate way and whispered a few words to the conductor, who was positively beaming. After what seemed ages of sinister silence the official turned towards us and pointing his finger at me declared impressively:

"There she is, the careless citizeness Keller-Skariatina, who unfortunately will have to go back to Russia right away."

"I'll come for you in a few minutes," our conductor added cheerfully, evidently in the very best of spirits.

Then they both went out of the room leaving me stupefied with consternation.

In a minute my companions surrounded me, loudly expressing their sympathy, which was really quite sincere now that they themselves were no longer involved in any trouble I had brought on them.

"You poor little thing," exclaimed the elegant lady, delicately embracing me.

"Oh, how awful," cried the young girl.

"Never mind, I am sure they won't put you in prison," consolingly said my kind, dark-eyed young woman of the first compartment.

The men were silent but from the expression of their faces I could see that they all were truly concerned about me.

"May we have a word with you in private?" I suddenly heard the violinist ask me. He had been conferring with his wife in a corner and beckoned me to join them.

"How much money have you?" they inquired when I came up to them.

"Fifty dollars given to me by the American Relief," I answered.

"In American money?"

"Yes."

"That's splendid," exclaimed the violinist, "splendid. Now listen to me and do as I tell you. You go and speak to that official privately in his office and beg him to let you continue your journey. If he refuses, just put a dollar on his table in the most casual way and then leave the room. I bet you anything that he'll let you through."

"Oh, but that's bribery!" I answered dubiously. "It may only make him very angry and hurt my cause all the more."

"Don't you believe it!" retorted my new friend,

[33]

while his wife nodded her head in support of his words. "This man and the conductor are evidently hand in glove in some crooked scheme and probably hold up one passenger out of every group that passes through here. The conductor must have known that you have some American money and told the official. Now a dollar means thousands here and I am perfectly sure that they'll let you through. Anyway you've nothing to lose for they are sending you back to Russia right away. So do as I tell you and you'll say 'thank you, Mr. X' when you see me again."

"Please, please do as my husband tells you," begged his wife. "He is really a very wise man and I always trust his judgment in serious matters."

Still I hesitated. It was bad enough to be sent back after all the trouble I had had to get out, but it would be worse still if they arrested me for bribery. But the violinist and his wife were pushing me towards the door and as I found myself in the corridor I suddenly felt courageous enough to take the risk. Before I could change my mind I ran towards a door marked "Office," and knocked.

"Come in," answered a man's voice, and the next instant I was alone with the chief himself. "What do you want?" he asked gruffly.

"Please, oh, please, won't you allow me to continue my journey?" I pleaded nearly frantic from excitement. "I had to have thirty-nine different permits to leave Russia, and they're all in good order, all except the visa that you say is one day overdue. I really did not notice that and am so sorry it happened. But for the sake of the other thirty-eight papers that are all right won't you let me go on? Oh, please, please!" I implored—"And you see," I continued, as he sat in silence staring at me, "if I return, by the time I straighten out the date of the passport the other thirty-eight permits will be overdue and then it will take me months and months to get new ones. I have been very ill and am still very weak."

"What do I care about your illnesses and permits?" he cried angrily. "All I know is that your papers should be in perfect order when you cross my frontier and I cannot let you pass if one of them is valueless. Get out of here and be ready in fifteen minutes to follow your conductor back to Russia."

Defeated and miserable I left his office. But there in the corridor my friends were standing anxiously awaiting the result of my interview.

"Well?" they both asked in one breath, "well, did you do it?"

"No, I couldn't, he was so angry. He wouldn't listen to me," I sobbed.

"But that's exactly the time when you should have put your dollar on the table! Why, you stupid, stupid little thing. Go right back and do it; otherwise in ten minutes you'll be on your way to Russia and maybe—prison."

"Here," said the violinist's wife, giving me her vanity case. "Don't cry—powder your nose, take one of your dollars along and go right in. Leave the rest with us so that you won't be tempted to give him more and go, for Heaven's sake—go!"

Too desperate to protest I obeyed and handing them the forty-nine dollars started once more towards the office, wiping my eyes and powdering my nose as I went, while in one hand I clutched the dollar bill. At the door I stopped and knocked again.

"Come in," called the same voice. I reëntered the office and faced the official for the second time. "Now what's the matter, didn't I tell you to get ready to leave in fifteen minutes? Ten minutes are up, you'll have to leave in five!"

"I—I . . . just came to say good-by," I stammered idiotically and then with a feeling of tumbling into a pitfall, thrust the dollar onto the man's table and rushed out of the room.

Trembling and gasping I joined the violinist and his wife who, hearing that I had taken their advice, patted me on the shoulder and promised consolingly that everything would be all right. We returned to the dining room where evidently my misfortune was being heatedly discussed, for when we came every one stopped talking and looked at me with sympathy and pity.

"Come on now, have another cup of tea," the violinist said persuasively, while his wife filled my plate with some more food. But I couldn't swallow a mouthful. Choking with excitement I sat on the edge of my chair expecting every minute to see the conductor reappear and hear him order me back to Russia.

Ten minutes passed in this suspense, then the door opened and the official appeared on the threshold and without looking at me or any one else in particular announced loudly:

"As I was sorry for the citizeness whose passport was overdue and wished to help her out of her trouble, I telephoned the chief authorities and asked them whether they would be lenient in this case and allow her to continue her journey. They were very kind and forgiving about the matter and, taking into consideration the fact that her passport is only one day overdue, have made an unusual exception and given her permission to proceed, together with the other eighteen passengers."

I could hardly believe my ears and did not dare look at any one for fear of showing my relief too clearly. But the violinist bent over me whispering congratulations and his wife put her arms around me and kissed me.

"Here are your forty-nine dollars," she murmured the minute the man had disappeared again. "Now, aren't you glad you listened to us? You see the reason we knew what to do was because we were warned by a friend before leaving Petrograd that such a thing might happen and were fully prepared for it. Just because your passport was overdue you happened to be the victim this time. And I don't believe that that man ever telephoned any authorities. But who cares? You're safe now and that's the main thing!"

I do not know whether I expressed my gratitude sufficiently to the violinist and his wife but as the French say I certainly owe them "une fière chandelle," perhaps for my life and undoubtedly for my freedom.

From the customs house we were taken to the quarantine building, for all the borderland countries were very much afraid of the contagious diseases that we might bring to them from Russia, and insisted that every Russian be put into quarantine for two weeks before entering their country. And no wonder, for at that time dysentery, typhus, cholera and even the plague, not to mention all the other, more usual, illnesses, were spreading over Russia, due to the famine and frightful living conditions.

The quarantine building was a large wooden structure, extremely clean and shining, and reminded one of a well-kept sanitarium for patients of small means.

There were no private rooms—at least I did not see any—but six or eight people were put together in one fair-sized airy room with decent beds and clean linen. As soon as we arrived we were again separated into two groups and then taken to the Baths where once more as in the Russian customs, we were stripped of all our clothes which were then carried away to be disinfected. We were ordered to take showers and scrub ourselves as well as we could. It took a long time to disinfect our clothes, and having bathed and bathed we finally sat down on little wooden benches, waiting for our things to be brought back. Luckily the bathroom, though very spacious (it could easily have contained fifty people), was beautifully warm and we did not shiver and sneeze as in that dismal place where we were stripped and searched at the Russian border. But when our clothes finally did appear and we began to dress— shrieks of dismay suddenly filled the place, for to our horror nearly every article had hopelessly shrunk. My black knitted dress was a sight, with the sleeves half way up my arms and the skirt nearly up to my knees. My hat refused to be pulled down and perched jauntily on top of my head, while my boots that had already been in a woeful state of dilapidation, had now wide cracks all over them and were turned up at the toes, quite in the Chinese manner.

Hopelessly we stared at each other. But it was of no

use to protest or lament, for the damage had been thoroughly done without any possibility of repairing it, and the only thing left was to resign ourselves to the fate of looking like the worst scarecrows that the world had ever seen.

Then we all burst out laughing and laughed and laughed till our sides ached and the tears ran down our cheeks. Even the attendants smiled though they kindly assured us that after all we did not look *quite* as bad as some of their former victims. That hardly seemed possible, but we tried our best to believe them and filed out of the Bath establishment, limp and weak from laughter.

The men gasped when they saw us and we gasped at the men! It was like the meeting of two groups of caricatures come to life; all we needed was some music and a sort of Apache dance to make it seem complete.

After being bathed and disinfected we were taken to the doctor and given a thorough medical examination; then again we were sorted out and shown to our respective rooms. Exhausted I lay down on my bed and fell asleep. . . . I must have slept for quite a while, for it was nearly dark when I awoke. At first I thought I was all alone; then I noticed a woman sitting near the window.

"What time is it? Where is everybody?" I asked,

jumping up and trying to recognize the figure by the window.

"They are all in the dining room having supper," softly answered an unknown voice, "but the doctor thought that it would be better for you to rest as much as possible, so I'll bring you your supper in here."

As the speaker came up to me I saw that she was one of the quarantine attendants, a pleasant, middle-aged woman, dressed somewhat like a trained nurse. Suddenly a terrifying thought flashed through my mind.

"Oh, I'm not developing any alarming symptoms, am I?" I cried frantically, "cholera or the plague or something of that kind?"

But she smiled reassuringly and patted my hand.

"No, no, you're all right," she said, "don't worry— I'll bring you a nice supper and then you'll feel quite well."

"But I don't want to eat," I answered, still suspicious and worried. "Couldn't you stay with me and talk a little?"

"That is just what I have been wanting to do for several hours," she said seriously. "Ever since I saw your name I have been wanting to talk to you. Tell me, did any of your relatives pass through here last year?"

"My mother was here," I answered excitedly, "she was in this very same quarantine exactly a year and a half ago. Let me see. This is October 1922, and she stayed here for two weeks in April 1921. Why do you ask me? Did you know her?"

"Yes," she replied gently. "I knew her quite well. She occupied this same room and this very same bed. When I saw your name I thought you might be her daughter, there is a strong resemblance, too, you know, and I purposely gave you her bed. She was such a lovely, gentle soul—so ill and yet so patient and brave—I'll never forget her. Do you know that when she arrived we had to carry her up to bed for she was too weak to walk? At first we were afraid that she would pass away without ever reaching "the Promised Land," as she always called England, but after a while she grew stronger and insisted that she could go on to Reval, even though we all tried to persuade her to remain with us a little longer. She spoke of you a great deal and told me that you would join her in England as soon as you could escape from Russia. She wrote you a letter too— I remember that so well because I had to help her write it—she was so weak. Did you ever get that letter? And before she left she gave me this—I always wear it."

She pointed to a small sapphire pin that I immediately recognized. It was a pin that my mother had worn the day she left Petrograd and miraculously it had not been taken away from her at the border! Somehow the sight of that familiar old pin that I had known ever since I could remember un-nerved me completely and throwing myself face down on my pillow I began to cry desperately.

"So she never got to her 'Promised Land'?" whispered the woman softly, stroking my hair.

"No," I gasped, "no, she died in Reval a week after she left you . . . that is why I am going there; to see her grave, and perhaps I'll die there too—I hope so."

Suddenly I felt two arms around me while a crooning wave of Esthonian speech flowed over my head. I could not understand one single word she was saying, but never did anything sound more soothing and persuasive. It made me think of a very old woman who lived with us in the country for years until she died. Her name was Minnie—Minnie Petrovna we called her —and she had been my aunt's nurse. I never knew exactly what her nationality was, Swedish, Norwegian or Finnish, but the quarantine woman's speech in a flash reminded me of her, and for a few minutes the years seemed to roll away. . . . I was a very small girl once again while I listened to Minnie Petrovna crooning over me in a strange language that I could not understand. "Rina 'Ladimoy" she always called me, unmercifully mispronouncing my name (Irina Wladimirovna) and strangely enough something the Esthonian was saying sounded also like "Rina Ladimoy." Every day at the same hour until she died (I must have been about seven years old then), old Minnie would come to see me in my nursery, her stick thump-thumping as she came down the long corridor, her gold bracelets jingling and her heavy silk dress rustling loudly at every step she took.

"There comes Minnie," my English nurse Nana would say, glancing at the clock and remarking, "She is on time to-day," or, "She is a few minutes early," or else, "She's a little late."

Closer and closer would sound the thumping and the jingling and the rustling and then Minnie would stand on the threshold smiling and greeting us in her broken Russian.

"And how is little Rina Ladimoy to-day?" she would invariably ask, while Nana thanked her politely in her own Russian that was just as bad as Minnie's, and told her the nursery news of the day. Sometimes Minnie would come in when I was still crying over a spoonful of castor oil or a broken doll, and then she would put her arms around me and croon in her strange language words that proved magically soothing. And as I lay on the small hospital-like bed in quarantine the old magic worked and dulled the pain.

I was not kept long in quarantine; in fact they let me out first, though they detained all my other fellow travelers. For what reason they made that exception in my favor I do not know. Perhaps as I was so weak they were afraid that I would die there and wanted to get rid of me before that happened. However, that does not sound very probable, for after all a quarantine is the right place in which to die! So there must have been some other reason.

The journey from quarantine to Reval was uneventful, and my first entry in my new diary that I somewhat grandiloquently entitled "The Diary of an Exile" says:

"It seems so strange to be traveling in peace, without any danger of arrest and imprisonment. No one pushes, no one shouts, no one threatens. . . . At first I looked in terror at the conductor, expecting him any minute to start yelling at me, but he is so polite and well mannered that I can hardly believe my eyes and ears. Then also I am so comfortable alone in a small compartment, and am not hungry any more. Altogether it is all too good to be true!"

II

O N arriving in Reval I went to a modest little
hotel where I looked up the address of Mr.
and Mrs. Wladimir Hvolson, and as soon as
I had bathed and tidied my strange looking clothes, I
went to call on them. I was anxious to see them without
delay, for they were the wonderfully kind people who,
though not personally acquainted with my mother, had
heard of her coming and had met her at the train when
she arrived from quarantine and actually taken her to
their own home. Then, seeing how desperately ill she
was they had immediately transferred her to one of
the best hospitals in Reval, the "Diaconissen Anstalt,"
where she remained for a whole week until the day
she died. Together with a friend of my family, Count

Alexis Ignatieff, they then had taken charge of her funeral.

As I am writing this I have on my table before me all the official papers concerning her illness and death: the hospital record, the doctor's certificate, the undertaker's statement and newspaper clippings from the *Revaler Bote*. And as I look at those papers (written in May, 1921—exactly 10 years ago) that describe her poverty more eloquently than any words could, I cannot yet realize that they are about my own mother and that she actually died there—on the threshold of her "Promised Land"—an exile, alone among kindly strangers who took care of her for charity's sake, and without one member of her family by her side.

"God's ways are not our ways, and I shall never travel any further," she wrote me a few hours before her death. Evidently she knew full well that her end was near, but that it should have been that way seems so strange and so unreal to me!

Exceptionally beautiful and sweet and gentle, she was one of God's loveliest creations, and her old age should have been spent in the surroundings of beauty that she loved so much and that formed such an appropriate background for her. Our old country place Troitskoe, with its great park and terraces and flower gardens was the right setting for the closing scene of her mortal existence, and it was there, among the roses that had surrounded her for more than forty-five years of her married life, and on one of those absolutely perfect summer days only to be seen in Russia, that she should have passed away.

This was what I was thinking about as I walked down the streets of Reval on my way to the Hvolsons', and I was so absorbed in my thoughts that I quite forgot how queer I looked in my extraordinary clothes, and only the stares of passers-by suddenly reminded me of my sorry plight.

By the time I had reached the Hvolsons' door I was so self-conscious about my looks that I hesitated before ringing their bell. Then, just as I had mustered sufficient courage to ring, the door suddenly opened and a nice-looking elderly man appeared, evidently on his way out.

"Excuse me, please," I asked shakily, "but could you tell me if the Hvolsons are at home?"

"I am Mr. Hvolson," he answered pleasantly, "may I ask who? . . ."

"I am Maria Mihailovna Skariatina's daughter," I managed to reply. And then because I was still so weak and could not properly control myself, I began to cry.

"Maria Mihailovna's daughter," exclaimed Mr. Hvolson, "why, bless my soul!" And, "bless my soul!" he repeated excitedly, as he led me into his house.

The next minute I was seated in a comfortable arm-chair, while kindly people bustled around me, covering my shoulders with a warm shawl, bringing me a glass of wine, ordering hot tea, and saying all the comforting things they could think of.

Later in the day after I had rested, Count Ignatieff came to see me and then told me all the details of my mother's illness and death.

"To-morrow I shall take you to her grave," Mr. Hvolson said, "but to-day you must rest, and then if you allow me to say so," he continued, with a kindly twinkle in his eye, "you might buy yourself a few new clothes."

Red with shame at the reminder of my shocking appearance I eagerly agreed. That afternoon I shopped for the first time in five years! A plain black woolen dress, some underwear, a pair of sturdy shoes, a hat, gloves and a small suitcase—these were my first purchases in exile. As all I possessed in the world was $44 of the $50 given me by the American Relief, I shopped as warily as possible, buying only the very cheapest things I could find. Even so, my dollars dwindled alarmingly and aghast I secretly counted and recounted them over and over again, wondering if ever I would be able to reach my sister's home in London with such an appallingly small amount of money. As though they guessed my thoughts my new friends inquired that evening about the state of my finances and were horrified when I finally told them.

"Oh, you must allow us to lend you twenty-five pounds," Mr. Hvolson cried, "we cannot let you travel with what you've got."

"But," I protested, "how will I ever repay you so much money? It's impossible—I cannot take such a sum. My sister is too poor to help me and heaven knows whether I'll ever find any work in England."

But they would not give in and we argued for a long while. At last we compromised on ten pounds. I hated to take any money from them for I realized that they were anything but well off. However it seemed to be the only reasonable thing for me to do.

The next morning I drove with Mr. Hvolson to the cemetery and found my mother's grave beautifully situated on top of a wind blown hill with a fine view towards the sea. A plain white wooden cross bearing her name in black painted letters marked the spot where she lay, and despite the fact that it was late autumn, flowers grew in profusion over her grave. Thus once more I had a proof of the Hvolsons' thoughtfulness, for they had managed to arrange her grave as attractively as they possibly could under the most trying circumstances.

Soon after we reached the place Mr. Hvolson, at my request, left me there alone for the day promising to return for me at nightfall. At noon, however, he quietly came back bringing some sandwiches and a bottle of milk, which he deposited next to me without saying a word and then went away again. All that day I sat on the grass by the grave dreamily thinking of my mother's life, of my own in connection with hers, of her unspeakable suffering during the Revolution, of her last tragic journey that ended here in this Esthonian cemetery, and of my pilgrimage to her grave.

Had she died under normal circumstances in Troitskoe, she would have been buried in my father's family vault beneath the little red brick cemetery church, or else in the Lobanov or Paskevitch vaults, both belonging to her family; the first on her father's side, the second on her mother's. And in either one of those burial places she would have had an elaborate marble or granite grave-stone, with golden Icons above it, glimmering softly in the red light of bejeweled lampadas.

But as I sat there dreaming a strange sensation crept over me, as though without words she were trying to tell me that she actually preferred lying out there in the open under God's own sky and with only the grass and the flowers above her, preferred it infinitely to the dark, damp vaults, with their heavy marble monuments and their dim, flickering artificial lights that could not compare to the glory of the sun and the moon and the stars.

"And then," she seemed to continue, "don't forget there is the wind that blows over my grave; sometimes it merely rustles, sometimes it rages and roars, and I like that too, oh, so much better than the shivery little draughts that are in all those vaults. And there's the rain that penetrates through the sweet smelling soil and causes life to stir all around me. . . . So you mustn't be sorry that I am not lying in state beneath a grand monument with my name on it in letters of gold —this is so much much better and I am glad to be here! So glad!"

And as these soothing thoughts entered my mind a feeling of peace invaded me and I fell asleep on the grave. I was still sleeping when Mr. Hvolson came for me, just as the sun was setting and the evening wind swept gently over the grass. Before leaving I put on the grave a handful of the soil that I had brought with me from Russia, and then having nothing else to give— no wreaths or flowers or anything customary, I pulled out some of my hair, and digging a little hole in the grave, buried my hair in it. Then with a pencil I wrote a few words on the cross. "Come unto me all you who are weary and heavy laden and I shall give you rest." After that I was ready to go and we left the cemetery in silence.

Ten years have passed since then and I have not been able to return there again.

Next day I said good-by to the Hvolsons and left for England via Germany and Belgium. As I entered the compartment where my seat was, I had another proof of how small the world is, for there was sitting an old acquaintance of mine—Count A. Mandteufel, with whom as a girl I used to dance at balls and whom I had not seen for years. Though I had known him but slightly, it was nice to find an acquaintance and we talked and talked until it was time for him to get off. After that two men came into the compartment, then later on a young woman and they turned out to be pleasant companions, too. When night came we at first decided to arrange ourselves so that the men would sleep on one bench and we two women on the other, but the young woman found better accommodations for herself in the next compartment, so that I had the entire bench all to myself, an unheard of luxury that had not come my way since pre-revolutionary days.

In Berlin I parted from my traveling companions, who were not going any further, and was amazed to hear that the two men were bolsheviks of importance whose names were quite familiar in Russia. But whatever they did at home as militant bolsheviks, as train companions, traveling incognito, I must say they behaved extremely well and had the nicest manners possible.

However, a few months later while I was still in

England an amazing tale reached my ears, a tale evidently started by the young woman of our traveling group. It told that I was assuredly a communist because I had been on amicable terms with the two important bolsheviks—my train companions—and that they had both even kissed my hand when they said good-by on the platform. And when I protested and tried to explain to the person who was so eagerly telling me this story about myself that I did not know those men were bolsheviks until they named themselves in Berlin, just as they were going away, I could see that she did not believe me though she politely said:

"Of course, of course."

In Berlin, as I had to wait a few hours before the departure of my train, I left the station and wandered about the streets, feeling like a ghost that had returned to familiar haunts—the Friedrichstrasse, Unter den Linden, and the shops where in former days I had had such fun buying presents for every one at home. And as I stood gazing into one of those shop windows I caught myself actually "shopping" in my mind and wondering whether my little son would like the fuzzy toy animals, or if my father would care for such a picnic basket or my mother be pleased with that green velvet traveling rug. Mechanically I looked at the prices and then with a start woke up from my day dream, half laughing at my stupidity, half crying at the pain of awakening.

"They're all dead, and you yourself are nothing but a ghost—a poor ghost at that, with only a few pennies left in the whole world," I admonished myself severely as I moved away from the shop window.

A woman who had been standing near me also window-shopping stared at me curiously; then impulsively putting out her hand said warmly in German:

"You're a war widow, nicht? So am I. It's pretty awful, but we've got to carry on—that's life."

And without waiting for my answer she turned away abruptly and disappeared in the crowd.

Aimlessly I continued walking until I found myself in front of the Hotel B. where in former days I had always stopped. For some reason I felt like seeing the place again, and slowly entered it and sat down in the lounge. No, it had not changed at all; the entrance, the lounge, the furniture—everything was the same—and I thought I even recognized the same faces. Suddenly I felt awfully tired while a wave of misery swept over me. What right had I, a shabby ghost, to be here among the living and of what use was it to awaken old memories and hurt myself so unnecessarily? After all, as the woman had just said, the only thing left for us was to carry on, and that is what I should be doing, not deliberately opening old wounds. Two great tears rolled down my cheeks and fell onto my lap. . . .

"Does Madame reside in this hotel?" a polite voice quietly asked me and looking up I saw a man, probably one of the managers, standing beside me.

"Why, no, no," I answered confusedly, jumping up and overturning the chair. "No, I do not live here, but I used to," I added, trying to smile and not succeeding.

"Well, in that case I am afraid Madame . . ." continued the manager still very politely, but rubbing his hands and bowing somewhat nervously.

In a flash I remembered my shabby appearance and understood what he was trying to tell me and before he could say it started to run towards the door. I thought I heard footsteps following me as I rushed into the street, and ran and ran until, breathless, I had to stop. But no one was following and with shaking knees and fast beating heart I walked back to the station, that appeared like a haven of safety after my miserable walk through the streets of Berlin. Luckily it was soon time to get on my train and with a sigh I sank onto the seat allotted me for my passage through Germany. There were three people in the compartment besides myself: a smart, well-dressed, well-groomed young woman, a typical old-fashioned, fat and red-faced hausfrau, and a very young girl who pleased me right away with her curly fair hair, blue eyes and wide jolly smile. At once the three busied themselves getting comfortably settled. The well-dressed woman took out of her elaborately fitted suitcase a pale pink silk traveling wrap, a pillow to match, a silver scent bottle and an uncut novel; the hausfrau unpacked a pair of roomy slippers which she immediately substituted for her sensible but heavy looking boots, then a home-made knitted cap to replace her hat, and a good-sized ham sandwich with some kind of a drink which she sipped directly out of a dark bottle; the young girl got out a pair of spectacles that made her look like a baby with grandma's glasses on, a well-thumbed copy book in which she immediately began to write and a box of peppermint lozenges that she consumed as rapidly as she wrote. Seeing every one so occupied I wanted to do something myself too and first wrote a little in my diary, then tried to read, but my head and eyes ached so badly that finally I gave up trying to do something profitable and began to look out of the window. Towns, factories, villages, farms and fields flashed by; endless fields with rich heavy soil that probably yielded splendid crops, but that somehow did not turn my thought to visions of peaceful agricultural life and pastoral arcadian scenes. For some reason they made me think of war, and of the hideous battlefields that I had seen with their dead and wounded and doomed men. And as the sun set and the shadows of evening crept over the great spaces that we were rushing through in the sickening way of German trains, swaying and swerving and smelling atrociously, it seemed to me that through the veil of dust I could see once again the grim outlines of heavy artillery, of endless processions of marching men, of rattling canteens and Red Cross outfits that I had once seen pass over fields as rich and fertile as these. Then it grew dark and the lamps went on in the train and I could not see anything more outside but a solid wall of blackness in which occasionally twinkled the lights in dwellings.

My companions began to eat but the smell of their food sickened me and I went out into the corridor and stood there for a while. When I came back they had finished eating and were talking in low tones with their heads close together. As I came in they instantly stopped their conversation which made me think that probably I was the subject of it. For some time we all sat in silence; then suddenly the girl addressed me with an irrepressible twinkle in her eyes.

"Pardon me, please," she said in a rather throaty but pleasant voice. "But do you mind telling us your nationality? You see, we all think differently and would be much obliged if you told us."

"I am Russian," I answered quietly, wondering how they would react to my information.

Instantly a change came over them: the young woman looked frightened, the hausfrau pursed up her fat lips and drew away, the girl stared at me with frank interest.

"A bolshevik, perhaps?" the young woman murmured fearfully, closing her silver-fitted traveling case with a snap and also edging away from me.

"Bolshevik or not, I don't care, but she's a Russian and I lost two sons on the Russian front," declared the hausfrau, looking at me with undisguised hatred, while her face twitched nervously and her hands locked and unlocked.

"I was only fifteen at the time of the war," the girl said meditatively, "and no one was killed in my family because father was too old to fight and brother too young, but I've heard all about it and read all about it so much that sometimes I believe I was actually there myself. It must have been thrilling!"

As I did not comment on their remarks, nor add anything to my first brief statement, the conversation dropped and silence reigned once more. Then suddenly the hausfrau, who had not ceased staring at me with eyes full of hatred, got up decidedly and taking her heavy old-fashioned bag along with her, went into the corridor. Soon after that the young woman rang the bell and asked the conductor to carry her suitcase out for her, and then as she followed him and closed the door behind her I heard them all three conferring in the passage. Though they were speaking in low tones I could hear enough to understand that both women were asking the conductor to give them other seats, one of them using the word "bolshevik" several times, while the other one repeated, "Russian, Russian."

"Jawohl, jawohl, ich verstehe," I heard the conductor say soothingly, and then he must have taken them to another compartment for the three moved away and all was quiet again.

The girl who had evidently been listening attentively to what the women were saying turned to me with an apologetic laugh.

"Silly fools!" she exclaimed indignantly. "One is afraid of you because she thinks that you might be a bolshevik and the other one hates you for being a Russian, but I don't care, I really don't," she added seriously and coming over to my side peered nearsightedly at me.

"You mustn't mind them," she continued, her eyes full of sympathy. "You see the old woman lost both her sons on your front and naturally hates all Russians, but you must understand and forgive her. As for the other one, well, she's only a scared "dumkopf" who probably thinks that a bolshevik is a thief and that her silver-fitted suitcase and her silks and laces and frills are not safe in the same compartment with you. But just forget her, that's all! And you see, I haven't run away and I'm glad to know you, really and truly. You may be a Russian, but our countries are no longer at war so you're not an enemy. And you're no bolshevik either, for a bolshevik would not look so frail and shabby," she added, blushing furiously.

Though I was feeling anything but happy after the past day's experiences, I had to laugh at that last point she made in my defense: "too frail and shabby to look like a bolshevik!" That was an original compliment, but at least one person had tried to say something kind about me. These bewildering new problems that had been cropping up ever since I left Russia were suddenly solved in my mind and the answer to them all was that Russians most decidedly were not popular abroad, at least not in this part of Europe. I wondered how it would be in England, though I began to realize that, whatever lay ahead there, I certainly was being put through a good school of training during this journey that would prepare me most efficiently for all the difficulties I was to meet in the future.

The rest of the way was uneventful. Safely I crossed the border, safely passed through the customs, marveling at the politeness of the Belgians who did not seem to mind that I was a Russian, and arrived at Ostend early in the morning in time to catch the boat to Dover. As the sea looked rather rough I cautiously breakfasted at the dock on tea and dry toast, while I watched with dismay a numerous British family seated at a table next to mine eat one of the biggest breakfasts I ever saw.

The father positively urged his brood to stuff as much as possible and even spoke quite sharply to his wife when she timidly tried to protest. As I left the table they were still eating stolidly and I could not help wondering how they would feel when they got to sea. Soon that question was answered, for immediately after leaving Ostend, the boat began to rock unmercifully and the first to feel the effects of the rocking was the numerous British family that unfortunately had settled down next to my deck chair. In order to get away from them and from other seasick passengers I wandered away and climbed on the boat deck. There, clinging to a small iron ladder, where during the entire crossing I remained poised like a figurehead on the prow of the vessel, I sang at the top of my voice, while the wind lashed my skirts and the rain beat stingingly in my face. It was wonderful up there away from everybody, alone with the rain and the wind and the sea, that made so much noise that I could not hear myself sing. And though I got soaking wet I never even noticed it until we landed.

III

IN Dover I shivered and shook and dried myself as best I could, but the amazing part was that I did not catch cold and never even sneezed after such a crossing in a November gale.

In the boat train to London I stared out of the window so as not to miss a single feature of my first glimpse of England. And as the countryside flashed by, it all seemed familiar to me as though I had seen it many times before. And as I gazed and gazed I seemed to hear old Nana's voice describing England over and over again, while I sat next to her on the big sofa in my nursery and pleaded, "Oh, some more, Nana, tell me some more," whenever she paused in her narrative. Yes, it all looked just exactly the way she had described it many years ago, and the word pictures that she had drawn were amazingly true to life.

"Some day you will go to England, Dickey Bird, to the land where the blue bells grow," she would say dreamily, "and then you'll remember all that I told you."

"But we'll go together, Nana," I would cry, throwing my arms around her neck, and then would sob bitterly when she answered softly, "No, Dickey Bird, you will go alone, for then I shall be lying low beneath the ground."

Painful impressions of childhood that hurt like little stabs, though years have gone by.

When the train came into London the first thing that struck me was the smell, the typical English smell that Nana always brought back with her in her trunks from London. The minute she opened those trunks (one, a little brown tin fellow, the other much larger, black, with a gold nail border and "Harriet Isabella Jennings" painted in red on top of it) I would catch the first whiff of that strange and wonderful smell that made my heart beat for some unknown reason that I could not have explained had any one asked me.

"The smell, the London smell has arrived!" I would shout, dancing excitedly around the trunks, while Nana unpacked her things and carefully sorted them. There would be gifts for everybody, no one was ever forgotten, and goodies, real English goodies that to this day I love so dearly. Plum puddings, mince meats, jams, and jellies—one by one she would unpack them as I stood by with breathless reverence and awe. The last time she went she brought me a silk Scotch tartan sash and a white satin picture frame with a gilt border.

Her trunks were the very first ones that I had ever seen in my short life, and to this day when I hear some one say "trunks," I instantly visualize Nana's little brown tin one and its larger black companion. Both sorrow and joy those trunks brought into my life; sorrow, poignant, tragic, heartbreaking, when Nana packed them before starting on her vacation to England, and joy beyond description when she unpacked them on her return. And as I stood on the platform in London, it seemed to me that I was standing by Nana's open luggage breathing in, with deep ecstatic breaths, my beloved London smell.

Though I had sent my sister a telegram from Dover announcing my arrival, for some reason it was not delivered until after I got to her cottage, and therefore, no one met me at the train. So after waiting a time and not knowing anything about subways and other cheap methods of transportation, I hired a taxi, to the detriment of my slender purse, and drove out all the way to Golder's Green* where Olga and her husband lived.

* "My Green," as Doctor Golder used jokingly to call it.

My first impressions were most cheering. I liked Golder's Green at once for it reminded me of my Kate Greenaway books, and I was fascinated with my sister's little cottage. But alas, a bitter disappointment was in store for me. I don't know why I had pictured to myself a room that would be my very own; a tiny room with a lattice window, a fireplace and two or three pieces of old-fashioned English furniture, including one of those quaint wash-stands with a large porcelain bowl and jug. Instead of that I was taken up to the one and only bedroom that the cottage possessed and kindly told that it would be mine until a suitable room could be found for me in some other Golder's Green cottage. Meanwhile Olga and George would sleep in the house of their friends the Millingtons. That was a terrible disappointment, probably because for months, ever since it had been decided that I would leave Russia and join my sister in London, I had dreamt about a little room all to myself that would at last mean home and peace to me, after the past homeless years. Ever since 1914, when I had left home and gone to live at the hospital where I worked and studied I had not had a room to myself, and in the last year the thought of such a room had become a veritable obsession.

More disappointments were in store for me next day when I saw how very poor Olga and George were and realized that I would be only an extra expense and burden to them. Though at first I could pay for myself I knew that the little money I still had would soon be gone and that unless I found some work right away I would have to be supported by them. That thought was intolerable and yet I was so tired, so desperately tired after all I had been through during the past years of war and revolution that the prospect of working so soon again terrified me. Then, of course, I could not think of occupying their bedroom for more than one night, and on the very first day of my arrival in England started to look for a room. Luckily the Millingtons offered to take me into their cottage and gave me a little bedroom for fifteen shillings a week, breakfast included. My suppers I was to have at my sister's, and in this way my new life in England was settled.

Soon I began to look for work, but at that time in the winter of 1922-23 it was extremely difficult to find anything to do, as first of all there was a great number of unemployed English men and women, and then also quantities of Russian emigrants who had arrived long before me and therefore were entitled to get work before I was. Gradually I became very depressed: my little room was cold and damp, my money was giving out, I could find no work. I would soon become a burden to my sister and I had no money to go to my little daughter who was then living with her grandmother in the south of France, ever since they had escaped from Russia in 1918. For five years I had not known whether she was alive or not and then when I came to England and heard that she was safe and sound, I had no money to go to her! In utter despair, this is what I wrote in my diary on November 22nd, 1922:

"I am writing again, because when I write I do not feel so unhappy. And I am so unhappy, so desperately, desperately unhappy. Everything is so hopeless and I constantly ask myself—why am I alive, and what have I to live for?

"But there does not seem to be any answer to that. Those that I loved best are dead; I have lost everybody and everything and have lived too long. My days are empty and cold and dreary, as though my life were dead too. What is the use of existing this way, and what awaits me in the future? Loneliness, poverty, misery, sickness, charity? Oh, if only I could end it all! I hoped so much to find rest here both for body and soul and to be able to forget the past. But that hope has turned out to be just a dream that can never come true, a castle in Spain that has vanished into thin air. Here as in Russia, there are the same petty worries about daily bread and work that is so hard to find. My money is all gone and I shall have to borrow three pounds from Olga, who has so little herself. . . . And then what? Borrow again and again 'ad infinitum'? No, that cannot go on long; I'd rather die. I am going to learn to write on a typewriter, but then will I find work when there are millions of unemployed here? And without money how can I go to Maia or bring her here? Even if I scraped up enough money for the journey, how can I ask her to share such poverty? Why did I ever leave Russia? It would have been so much better had I stayed there, for at least there I could have found some work in my hospital, or else the American Relief would have given me something to do, as interpreter, perhaps, or on their medical staff. And then again, even in that wretched room of mine, I had my own furniture, my own things . . . at least I slept in my own bed and had I fallen ill I would have gone to my hospital where our doctors and nurses would have treated me for nothing whereas here, if I fall ill, what will happen? Either Olga will have to pay my expenses or else I'll be a charity patient. It is all like a nightmare. How I wish I had never left Russia!

"Who could have thought that I would have the same kind of troubles here as over there? I am just as cold in my little bedroom, often I am just as hungry and as for my clothes—well, no one could be shabbier. And to think that I was looking forward to an entirely new outfit and gloating at the prospect of throwing away all my old rags. What an irony and what a disappointment! But life seems full of them. Of course Olga and George are very good and kind to me but the thought

[71]

of being a burden to them frightens me and then too, as Tourgeniev says: 'There is nothing sadder than to sit on the edge of a strange nest.' I try so hard to be cheerful and jolly when I am with them but when I am alone I cry all the time, even though I realize that crying does not help."

"I cannot see what awaits me in the future," I write a few days later. "I am blind, blind, and the only thing that helps is to remember the words 'I shall lead the blind down a new road and shall straighten out their way.' "

My feelings were a strange mixture those days. I loved London and Golder's Green, enjoyed taking long walks, sight-seeing, reading all I could about England so as to acquire as much of the English atmosphere as possible and was glad to have the companionship of my sister after all those years. On the other hand the fact that I had no money, no work, and was obliged to borrow from Olga, that I could not go to see my little daughter, that I was shabby and cold and often hungry, made me desperately miserable. It was as though life were made of the oddest jumble of sensations, when one minute I would be gloating delightedly over something typically English and the next tightening my belt and buying a bun to get rid of that hungry feeling. After having starved in Russia for nearly five years my body suddenly seemed to require an unusual amount of food and the Millingtons' breakfast and Olga's supper, though plentiful enough in ordinary circumstances did not seem to be able to satisfy my craving for more nourishment.

Shortly after I arrived I had an audience with the Dowager Empress Marie of Russia, who at that time was living in Marlborough House with her sister Queen Alexandra. Both my mother and father had been deeply devoted to the Empress all their lives since the days of their youth when she had come to Russia as Czarevna, and I knew that they would have wanted me to go to see her at once. Besides as former Maid of Honor it was my duty to ask for a presentation, so I wrote Countess Mengden, her Lady in Waiting and asked for one. On the appointed day, not having anything new to put on I brushed up my old clothes as best I could and sallied forth to Marlborough House, incidentally carrying my net marketing bag along as I intended to buy some food on the way back. However, soon after I left the subway I saw a stand with very tempting vegetables and apples at a remarkably low price, and not wanting to miss such an opportunity—bought all I could and continued to walk towards the palace with my net bag full of carrots and things. Arriving at Marlborough House I was stopped at the entrance by an imposing-looking individual and asked who I was, where I was going, and exactly whom I was intending to call on.

"I am the Countess Irina Wladimirovna Keller, and I have an audience with Her Majesty the Dowager Empress of Russia," I answered, with all the dignity I could command, hoping that the man would be duly impressed. But he merely looked suspicious and casting one more supercilious glance at my shabby clothes and net bag told me rather sharply to wait a minute while he telephoned. However, almost immediately he returned and with smiles and bows requested me to follow him across the courtyard to the main entrance. Here he turned me over to another resplendent individual who ushered me towards the elevator in a grave and stately manner, though out of the tail of his eye he too cast a few disapproving looks at my shoes and bag and vegetables. I was first received by Countess Mengden in her rooms, where I left my famous bag and then she took me to the Empress. I had not seen her since the winter of 1917 and was shocked to see how frail she had become. She kept me for more than an hour and was ever so kind to me, asking a great deal about the last years of my parents, about my own experiences during the Revolution, about my escape and laughed when I described my arrival at Marlborough House with a bag of vegetables. Then she told me many little stories about the days when she and my parents were young, told me how much affection she had for them and cried a little when I gave her a very old photograph of theirs taken together on the day they were betrothed.

"How well I remember them looking just like that," she said, smiling sadly. "Your mother was lovely, one of the loveliest women I ever knew, and your father was handsome too. And how well he played the piano! You know, we used to play four hands together quite often and then we skated and used to slide down the ice hills. That was very long ago and yet it seems only yesterday."

As I was taking leave of her, curtseying low and kissing her hand she embraced me warmly and then blessed me, saying, "I am doing this in memory of my old friends your dear parents, 'en souvenir de vos chers Parents,'" she repeated as, blinded with tears, I backed out of her drawing-room.

Later on she sent me her last photograph and wrote those very same words on it: "en souvenir de vos chers Parents." That photograph is standing on my table now.

Shortly after my first audience with the Dowager Empress I had an audience with her eldest daughter the Grand Duchess Xenia. She was lovely to me too and that winter I saw her quite often and learned to love her very much. At her house at Prince's Gate I met many old friends whom I had not seen for years, and it was delightful to meet them all again. Then too I became very fond of her Lady in Waiting Sofia Dmitrievna Evreinova, a perfectly charming woman. Altogether I spent many happy hours at Prince's Gate.

Every Saturday evening and every Sunday morning I used to take the bus from Golder's Green and drive down to London to the Russian church. The minute I crossed the threshold I would have the impression of being back in Russia again and everything else—Revolution, exile, England, London would be forgotten and fade away into the fantastic realm of events and places that had never existed except in imagination. At the right of the central aisle, a little ahead of every one, usually stood the Empress Marie, slender and erect despite her age, and Dowager Queen Olga of Greece in the trailing draperies she always wore, and Grand Duchess Xenia and other members of the Imperial family. And wherever I looked I saw the familiar faces of friends and acquaintances, some looking terribly poor and shabby, while others still managed to keep up appearances. After the service was over and the Empress had departed, the entire Russian colony of exiles would form congenial little groups outside the church, talking, exchanging news and arranging future meetings. Everybody spoke Russian, of course, and the impression of being in Russia continued until once more I found myself in the streets of London walking in the direction of the bus that took me back to Golder's Green.

In the first days after my arrival from Russia many of my compatriots, most of whom had left the country shortly after the Revolution, were anxious to hear all the news I could give them about Petrograd and seemed very disappointed and unbelieving when I described the political situation and expressed my firm belief that the Soviet government was becoming stronger every day. Most of the exiles had the wrong impression that any day the bolsheviks would be overthrown and that they would all be able to return to Russia and resume their old mode of living that had been broken off in 1917 and that they expected to take up again where they had left it as though there had never been any revolutionary interlude. Some of my compatriots were quite annoyed with me for not agreeing with them and even accused me of pro-bolshevistic tendencies. Time has now proved that I was right and ten years have passed without any overthrow of the new government.

I also had several offers to lecture and write about my experiences in Russia but as I had given my word to Dr. Golder that I would not do so for seven years (that being one of the conditions that the Soviet government had made when he asked for my release), I naturally refused all offers and did not speak in public nor write anywhere. Strangely enough two years later I received through Dr. Golder a message from a prominent bol-shevik—one of those who had signed the papers for my release, saying that he congratulated me for keeping my word and for being a "noble" woman indeed in the true sense of that word.

Though I could neither speak publicly nor write I was most anxious to do my share in Relief work as I knew so many people in Petrograd who were in desperate need of food and clothes. It was then that I got in touch with various Relief Associations and gave them all the names and addresses of those in Petrograd that I considered needed most help. Besides the American Relief Administration in Russia and the Nansen Relief, remarkable work was being done by a splendid English organization in the way of sending to Russia food parcels and clothes for the sufferers.

In those days I used to see quite often an old friend of my mother's, Lady Carnock, formerly Lady Nicholson, wife of Sir Arthur Nicholson, ex-Ambassador to Russia. Sir Arthur had been created Lord Carnock since his return from Russia—hence the change in their names. They lived in a charming house in Cadogan Gardens and there too I spent many delightful hours, for Lord Carnock had an unusually brilliant mind and his wife was the very soul of kindness. Of course we talked mostly of old days in Petersburg, when I was still a very young girl and used to see Lady Carnock in my mother's drawing-room. It was then (in the old days), around tea time usually, that the footman would come to the door of my schoolroom and announce gravely that Her Excellency requested my presence in the drawing-room. Hastily jumping up from my desk with apologies to the teacher of the hour I would brush my hair, wash my hands and race down the long corridor, slowing down to a sedate walk just as I entered the drawing-room. Here I would find my mother presiding at her small tea table, surrounded by guests. Gravely I would curtsey to each one separately, submit to kisses, answer the usual questions and then curtseying once more leave the drawing-room, walking as straight as an arrow and as demurely as I possibly could until I had reached the door. Once safely out of sight I would again scamper down the long dark corridor stamping my feet loudly in an ecstasy of freedom. Then at my schoolroom door I would slow down and enter in the approved manner. However, I would arrive gasping, my cheeks red, and my hair in wild disorder, to the displeasure of my governess who would invariably say:

"You have been running like a gamin! When will you learn to behave as a young lady should?"

Meekly I would apologize and after tidying my hair settle down once more to my lesson. Usually such an interruption would occur only once, but sometimes my mother sent for me again when a friend of hers arrived to whom she particularly wanted to show me. Though I was spoken to only in the stereotype manner over and over again by the ladies in my mother's drawing-room still I had my favorite ones and also those I disliked. Instinctively I knew which were sincere and which were not and accordingly either felt myself attracted or repelled. Lady Carnock decidedly attracted me as I realized her genuine kindness and sincerity from the very first time I met her. After I had made my début she gave a magnificent ball in my honor at the British Embassy where I enjoyed myself tremendously dancing for the first time in my life with a lot of English young men. One of them, a youth about my own age, even proposed to me at the end of the evening and seemed really chagrined when, thanking him for the honor, I answered decidedly, no. He kept writing to me for a long time afterwards and when I married sent me a little gold-fitted traveling case as a wedding gift. Like an old lady who lives in the past I smile reminiscently whenever I hear his name and wonder what his wife is like!

Besides the Carnocks I met many other interesting people that winter in London: Lady Muriel Paget, who during the war had been with her hospital in Petrograd and done such splendid work over there; Sir Bernard Pares; Mrs. Nesta Webster, the well-known authoress; Father Bell, secretary to the Archbishop of Canterbury; Father Napier Whittingham; the Tudor Poles and many others. I was even asked to meet Lord Curzon in

THE DOWAGER EMPRESS MARIE OF RUSSIA, A PICTURE
WHICH SHE SENT ME SHORTLY BEFORE HER DEATH

order to tell him all I knew about the political situation in Russia and also about the persecution of the Church, but on account of my promise to remain silent for seven years, I had to refuse the invitation. In a way life was extremely interesting in those days, and only when I found myself alone in my little bedroom did my misery return.

"I am so cold to-night, so cold," I write in my diary again. "Everything I touch in my room is like ice and the fog is creeping through the chinks in the window. I wish I could have a fire—but I can't! First of all the grate does not burn coal any longer but has been arranged for gas; then I would not dare disturb Miss Howe, the very grand maid, by asking her to build a fire, and last but not least I have no extra money to buy any coal with. So there: "un point c'est tout" as my governess used to say, and those are the reasons why I am freezing this very minute. It's a torment to undress in this room and a torment to try and get warm in bed for the sheets are cold and damp and the only possible way of sleeping is to wrap oneself up in a blanket just like we used to do in Russia during the Revolution. I tried using a hot water bottle but it gave me chilblains and once it leaked, making my bed sopping wet. At night time I am dressed in all kinds of queer things: a sweater, bed-stockings and even my old Orenburg shawl.* Often

* These had been sent to me from Russia by Dr. Golder.

like a stupid child I cry and cry from the cold. It was certainly worth the journey from Russia to suffer in the same way here!

"And I am hungry; right now this very minute I am hungry and have nothing to eat. I had an early supper in the 'Dairy Express,' and evidently did not have enough to carry me through the night. And I look shabbier every day: my one and only black dress is turning a reddish rusty hue and so is my hat, my heels are downtrodden, I have lost my umbrella and when it rains I look like a wet hen in my old fur jacket. I sleep badly and wake up many times with a start wondering what has happened. At first I do not realize what is the matter; then I remember and the anguish begins. Perhaps that shock of awakening, followed by the flood of painful memories and the full realization of what has happened, is the most tormenting part of all the twenty-four hours."

December 3rd

"Soon I must borrow from Olga again. I have spent three pounds in two weeks. That is much too extravagant and I must cut down my expenses."

December 10th

"My hair is falling like the leaves in autumn. If this continues there soon won't be a hair left on my head. Won't my rusty hat look nice 'on my bald pate?'"

"I have not felt well for some time and finally saw a doctor to-day. He said: 'No worries, plenty of rest and good food. And I recommend a trip to Italy!' He has made me positively hysterical with his sound advice. Why didn't he suggest a cruise on my private yacht?"

In December there was a Russian Bazaar organized by the society exiles in Chesham House, the former Russian Embassy. The Grand Duchess Xenia kindly asked me to sell at her table and I delightedly agreed. It was fun to be together with all my old friends and acquaintances in the big ball room of the ex-embassy, fun to help arrange the tables, fun to be back in a purely Russian atmosphere. The main object of the Bazaar was to sell one's own things that had been saved from the Revolution and then give a certain percent of the sale for the benefit of Russian Relief Charities. Jewels, laces, miniatures, gold, silver, enamel, bibelots and cigarette cases studded with precious stones, fans, little jade and crystal figures, paper knives, ash trays, frames, parasol handles (mostly made of semi-precious stones of the Ural Mountains)—such were the things for sale. Personally I brought several of my sister's possessions and a few little trinkets that Dr. Golder had kindly brought out of Russia for me. It was pathetic to see what hopes were built on the expected sale of these personal belongings, to notice the eagerness of the sellers, the anxious look in their eyes, the involuntary trembling of their hands—for the sale of each thing in most cases meant food and clothes and warmth and all the essentials of life, and then to witness the delight over a successful sale or the bitter disappointment when it was all over and many things had to be packed up and taken back home, until they reappeared at the next Bazaar. After several Bazaars we grew to know each other's possessions so well that we would ask anxiously, "Oh, where is your gold cigarette case, is it sold? Has any one bought the carnelian necklace? And what has become of the crystal elephant?"

And the agony of excitement with its climax of joy or despair when a prospective buyer approached the table and deliberately began to look the things over.

"Oh, please, God, please, God, please! Make him buy something," I would pray silently but frantically and nearly collapse when an object belonging to me would be noticed, touched, lifted and carefully examined.

"How much is this?" I would then hear a voice ask while I in a daze would shakily name the price.

"Very pretty indeed, I'll think about it," the voice would then continue, trailing away into nothingness as its owner drifted on towards the next table and then I'd feel that I could not stand it another minute but would have to burst into tears right there. But sometimes, though very rarely—only twice in my case—the voice would say, "Very pretty indeed, I think I'll take it," and then a flood of joy, fierce, primitive, indescribable joy would nearly sweep me off my feet at the realization that something good had happened at last!

Then a Russian ball was given at Chesham House and I had to face the problem of getting something appropriate to wear. But as not a penny could be spared for a new ball dress, I borrowed a plain black silk gown with shoes and stockings to match from my friend Elena Bobrinsky Boutourline. Not having been to a ball since the winter of 1914 I was as excited as a débutante and could hardly sit still in the subway train in which I rode to the ball. In my eagerness I ran all the way from the subway station to Chesham House and when I got there it all seemed like a dream: the beautiful Embassy, the Grand Duchess Xenia looking so lovely as she stood at the head of the stairs receiving the guests as they came up, the men and women in evening clothes, the music, the flowers, the perfume and my first waltz with my old friend General Hartman. And then something happened that shattered my dream to pieces. As I was floating blissfully to the strains of a popular old Russian waltz past the doorway where a group of people were standing watching the dancers, Princess Merika Galitzine tapped me on the shoulder.

"One minute please," she whispered, "I have something to tell you," and as I stopped dancing and joined her she kindly said, "You evidently forgot to put a slip on under your dress and one can see way down to your stomach on both sides when you lift your arms."

In terrible confusion I glanced around to see if any one else had noticed my indecent attire and saw that many people were looking at me and smiling in amusement. Red with shame and blinded with tears I rushed up to my partner whispering: "Please excuse me but there's something the matter with my dress," and then dashed down stairs to the dressing room where luckily there was no one. Throwing myself into a chair I burst into tears. It seemed too bad that the very first bit of pleasure that had come my way for nine years should end in such a disgraceful manner. Soon however I had to stop crying for other women came in and then, surreptitiously drying my tears I examined the state of my frock. It was terrible indeed, for undoubtedly it was supposed to be worn over a slip and had long slits on both sides that ran from the arm-pits to the waist. At the top of those slits there had evidently been snappers that had long ago come off, so that the only thing to do was to sew the slits up and that's what I did, stitching laboriously by the lamp. When my task was finished and the dress ready I put it on and went upstairs again but the fun had gone out of me and soon I left the ball and returned to my room in Golder's Green.

Another dreadful thing happened to me a few days later when I was invited to spend an evening at Madam Zinoviev's, *née* Baranoff. Dressed in an old brown velvet gown that had once belonged to my mother and that Olga had had remade for me I sallied forth that evening about eight o'clock in the direction of the bus that would take me very nearly to the Zinovievs' door. It was a pleasant warm night and I thoroughly enjoyed the walk through Golder's Green to the bus and then the drive on its top deck. Arriving at my destination I ran down the winding stairs, and just as the bus was preparing to start, jumped off the platform and before I could realize what was happening or prevent it landed right in the middle of a horrid-looking puddle. In dismay I stared at my shoes, wondering what on earth I'd do when suddenly I noticed nearby a plot of grass. Frantically rushing towards it and taking off both shoes I carefully wiped them over and over again on the grass. Then thinking that I had cleaned them quite well, I put them on again, walked up to the Zinovievs' house and rang the door bell. In the drawing-room, where many guests were already assembled, I was cordially greeted by my hostess and invited to sit down next to her on the sofa by the fire. But I had not been seated long when I began to notice a queer unpleasant smell that seemed to come from the direction of the floor at my feet. Suddenly, with a start of horror, I realized that it was my shoes that were smelling and that the heat of the fire was drying them and at the same time bringing out that terrible odor stronger and stronger every minute. Aghast I turned towards my hostess with the intention of explaining to her what had happened and of asking her to take me to a dressing room where I could wash my shoes properly and then perhaps wear a pair of hers while mine were drying, when to my dismay I saw that she was holding a perfumed handkerchief to her nose and making frightful grimaces at some one opposite her as much as to say: "I can't stand this another minute—it is too awful!"

For some reason that pantomime paralyzed me and for a few seconds I stared at her without being able to utter a word. Then before I knew what I was doing I jumped up off the sofa and gasping "good-by, and thank you for such a nice evening," ran out of the room and out of the house into the street. There, blindly I stumbled on forgetting about the bus and the direction in which I was to go until I had to stop from sheer exhaustion. When finally I came to my senses I discovered that I was practically lost and had to walk miles to find my Golder's Green bus. Once safely atop of it I began to cry, great tears of shame and mortification streaming down my cheeks, and I cried all night long, tossing and sobbing in a state of utter despair. I never explained to my hostess what happened and to this day she probably wonders what on earth was the matter with me.

Around Christmas time, wanting to buy a few gifts I decided to sell one of the jewels that had been saved and brought out of Russia for me—an aquamarine pendant in a diamond setting, attached to a thin platinum chain. At the advice of friends I took it one morning to a well-known jeweler and after walking past his great shop several times, suddenly made up my mind to go through with the unpleasant business and timidly entered the place. At the door I was met by a suave manager who smiled and bowed politely and asked me what I desired. Conquering my fright I answered as bravely as I could that I wanted a small jewel appraised as my intention was to sell it. Instantly the manager's suave smile disappeared, his back straightened up and with a lofty wave of his hand he briefly ordered me to follow him. Meekly I obeyed and with beads of cold perspiration on my forehead and the jewel tightly clasped in a clammy hand trotted behind him into a small sized inner room back of the store. Here I was told to wait while he went in search of somebody else. In a few minutes he returned accompanied by another man who without even glancing at me merely said:

"Well, where is it?"

"Here it is," I answered in a voice that certainly did

not sound like mine, while I tried to appear indifferent, probably without any success, as I handed him the pendant with trembling fingers.

"Hum," said the man, staring at it coldly, "hum, how much do you want for it? And," he continued, transferring his cold stare to my face and then letting it travel over my shabby clothes. "How did it come into your possession? You'll have to explain that, you know."

"Oh, I can easily tell you that," I cried, "I am a Russian, my name is Countess Irina Keller and I bought that jewel from Faberge the great Court jeweler in 1916."

There was a brief silence during which the men looked significantly at each other, then the manager, with a half smile that was anything but pleasant said: "Prove it, Madam, we need proofs."

For a minute I was at a loss what to do, wondering which friend I had better call up to prove my identity and to say that I was really speaking the truth. Then I decided to give Lady Carnock's name.

"Call her up," I said as haughtily as I could manage. "She'll tell you that I am Countess Irina Keller, and that you can believe me when I say that the jewel is really mine."

The manager disappeared again and soon came back asking me this time quite politely to speak to Lady Carnock who was on the telephone.

"Is this you, my dear?" came the sweet familiar voice over the wire, "after speaking to that man I was afraid that perhaps some one was impersonating you at the jeweler's, that's why I wanted to speak to you. I am so glad you thought of calling me; tell the man to speak to me at once!"

Evidently what she told him proved to be most satisfactory for after a short conversation with her the manager returned all smiles again.

"It's all right, Countess," he said, his shoulders nice and round again and his voice as suave as ever, "and you must forgive this little formality, but you see these days many strange things happen and naturally we have to protect ourselves."

"Naturally," I agreed, still trying to appear unconcerned and indifferent, but wishing desperately that I could dash through that dreadful store and disappear from it forever. But there was still the ordeal of having the jewel appraised and then bought or rejected to go through with. Alas, despite the smiles and bows and purrings of the manager I was offered only eight pounds and, being too frightened and upset to argue, accepted the money and leaving the aquamarine in the hands of the man walked out of that store—forever.

About that same time a delightful thing happened. The Millingtons, my landlords, kindly asked me to go with them to their cottage in "Hants" near Grayshot and spend the Christmas holidays there. I was over-joyed, as all my life I had wanted to see a real English Christmas, and accepted the invitation with enthusiasm. It was decided that I would drive down with them in the car hired specially for that occasion and stay as long as they did. My sister and her husband would come a few days later and live at a nearby inn. From beginning to end it was one of the nicest experiences I had in England and I shall never forget it. On the morning of our departure the car arrived bright and early and our suit-cases were tied firmly with ropes on top of it and back of it. When everything was ready we all excitedly got in: Mr. and Mrs. Millington, Miss Howe, Timmy the sealyham and myself. Through the suburbs of London onto the highway we went at what seemed to me, who had not ridden in an automobile for years, break-neck speed, but what probably was only a pleasantly reason-able pace, while I stuck my head out of the window firmly determined to see everything I possibly could. We passed through country villages and towns so typ-ically English that my breath was fairly taken away and I could have shouted aloud for sheer joy! Time flew only too quickly and I was amazed when the car, sud-denly slowing down and turning off the highway into a narrow lane, came to a full stop, and Mr. and Mrs.

Millington in one breath cried hospitably, "Welcome to our cottage, welcome!"

It was a lovely little place, of the kind one dreams about. Very old, possibly a hundred and fifty years or more, picturesquely situated on a slope with trees and bushes all around it—it made me think of the days of real old "Merrie England."

I was given a little room quite like the one I had been dreaming about for years, with white-washed walls and plain old English furniture. Through my window I could see the boughs of a splendid old pine tree and at night when the stars shone through those boughs, the picture that that window framed was so lovely that I would sit up in my small bedstead and watch and watch it until my eyes closed and I'd fall asleep. Everything in that cottage was full of charm—the bedrooms on the upper floor, the parlor downstairs where there was a great fire-place in front of which we always had our meals, the kitchen and every nook and cranny. Just outside there was an old-fashioned well, where every day I helped Mr. Millington pump the water up by hand, and a garden shed where he kept his tools and pottered away for hours. The country all around was beautiful and I used to take long walks exploring in all directions. Not far off was the famous Devil's Punch Bowl, an immense area where the ground had sunk in the shape of a gigantic bowl, and the Broom Squire's Cottage, called that because for more than two hundred years its owners had made brooms. The village itself was a quaint old place and often I would go down to its one and only store and buy bull's eyes and other sweets. Christmas was spent in real English fashion and I remember vividly how beautiful the church bells sounded as they pealed merrily at mid-night. Church services, Christmas carols, Christmas dinner and Yule log—the program was complete and I saw and heard and tasted and smelt it all with the feeling that I was living in the days of Mr. Pickwick and Mr. Pecksniff. Again time flew by only too quickly and I was heartbroken when the day came to return to London and my little room in Golder's Green.

In January a stroke of good luck came my way. Prince Serge Dolgorouky needed some important documents translated and offered me the opportunity of helping him. As the papers were written in all kinds of ancient languages—Slavonic, Greek and others—I had to spend a great deal of time in the Reading Room of the British Museum and liked that tremendously, for my work was congenial and also I met there quite a number of extremely interesting people. The chair I usually occupied stood between those of an elderly Japanese professor and of a young Hindu student, both of whom I got to know quite well. The Japanese was a real philosopher and after working for hours we would go outside the museum and talk at length on all kinds of abstract subjects. His ideas and point of view on life seemed to help me a great deal and I used to look forward eagerly to our almost daily discussions. The Hindu student was a lovely girl who looked on the world with great soulful eyes and always wore her national costume. She was quite a philosopher too and often joined us on the portico of the museum and, calm and dignified, expressed her views in grave, measured, harmonious words. Several times she asked me to her rooms and there, to the accompaniment of a peculiar long instrument with strings called a citar, she sang in a rather deep and beautiful voice many Hindu songs. In a way their melody reminded me of our Russian folk songs and not only their melody but the way she sang them too, which after all is quite natural when one takes into consideration the neighborhood of Russia and India. Often at home in Troitskoe I used to listen to the songs of the peasants, singing in the garden, singing in the fields, always singing whether at work or play, mostly mournful, long drawn out melodies though sometimes they would burst into something gay, and then afterwards I would write down those songs and play them on the piano. I collected quite a number that way and strangely enough two of the Hindu songs were absolutely like two Russian melodies that I had once written down. Then besides our folk

[95]

songs the Hindu and I had another bond in common—our love for Rabindranath Tagore. She would often recite his poems and then as I closed my eyes and listened it would seem that a magic carpet, defying time and space, had brought me back to my mother's favorite bench in her rose garden where she used to sit and read for hours the poems of Tagore. All her life, from the day she was sixteen until the very end, she used to write down in a special book all the thoughts that pleased her most in every book she read and a few days before her death in Reval she wrote on one of the last pages the words of Tagore: "Peace, my heart, let the time for the parting be sweet. Let it not be a death but completeness."

I was sorry when my work was finished and there was no more reason to go daily to the British Museum. But though I had no longer any special purpose for going there, still the attraction was too great and often I used to find myself back in my old chair or be much perturbed when some one else got hold of it before I did. Serge Dolgorouky paid me very well, twenty-five pounds, for my work and again I was able to be independent and not borrow from Olga any more. At the same time I found another room in a cottage on my sister's street, Addison Way, and this is what I wrote in my diary shortly after moving: "I am so pleased; I have discovered such a nice little room at seventeen shillings

MY MOTHER AT A FANCY DRESS COURT BALL

a week in a cottage not far from Olga. Its walls are painted a bright pink, it has a real fire-place where my landlady lights a fire every day, a big shiny brass bedstead with a white and pink cover and a comfortable wicker arm chair. The window is wide but has no chinks and is situated on the sunny side of the house. There's lots of sun in the room and it looks ever so gay and bright. Right under it is the kitchen and therefore my floor is nice and warm. Since I have moved I sleep well as I am no longer cold, and then too, having been paid for my work, I eat well and am no longer hungry, which is such a comfort. The past weeks were pretty bad when I had only three shillings a week for lunches and extras between the Millingtons' breakfast and Olga's supper, but now everything is all right and I am really and truly comfortable.

"I have no pictures on my wall but one which I cut out of a newspaper entitled 'The Spirit of Spring' and have pasted over my fireplace. I love it; it is full of movement and life and the promise of better things."

But though I was rich with my twenty-five pounds still I tried my best to find some work and nearly every day answered advertisements and applied for jobs. But wherever I went I seemed to be too late, probably because I lived so far away in Golder's Green and London girls always got in ahead of me, and situation after situation would tantalizingly pass me by. Once I remember stopping at Lady Carnock's with an advertisement that I had just clipped out of the newspaper. It said that an elderly blind man wished to engage in the capacity of secretary the services of a young woman under thirty-five of pleasing appearance and gentle manners, or words to that effect. Hoping to qualify I was on my way to see him and proudly displayed the clipping to Lady Carnock announcing my intention of applying for the position. I was much disappointed when she threw up her hands in dismayed protest.

"But, my dear, you cannot go there," she exclaimed, "there's something wrong about it! Why should a blind man want as secretary a young woman of pleasing appearance when he cannot see what she looks like? No, you must promise me that you won't go to him." And seeing her so upset I promised.

Several times I went to Parliament, thanks to Lord Carnock, but one day not having a pass and yet wanting very much to hear the speeches that were to be about Russia, I went there hoping that I would have the luck of meeting some acquaintance who would help me to get in. However I did not see any one I knew downstairs and was standing disconsolately thinking that the only thing for me to do was to go home, when suddenly a nice-looking man came up to me and politely asked if there was anything he could do.

"My name is Mardy Jones of Pontipried and I am

a member of Parliament," he said, "and seeing you stand there looking somewhat lost, if I may say so, I thought that perhaps I might be of some assistance."

"Oh, yes," I cried delightedly, "if you're a member of Parliament you can certainly help me! I have no pass and yet I do want to hear the speeches about Russia. I am a Russian, you see, and my name is Irina Skariatina Keller," I continued, producing as evidence my English pass-port that I always carried around with me in my handbag. "I have been to Parliament several times, thanks to English friends, but forgot to ask them to give me a pass to-day. Do you think you could arrange for me to get in?"

"Of course," answered Mr. Jones gallantly, "of course I can get you in." And in a few minutes everything was arranged and I was up in the gallery, listening to one of the most interesting speeches on Russia that I ever heard. Once my Parliamentary host came up to see if I was all right. And although I never saw him again I must say that he was one of the most obliging men I ever met.

Sometimes I used to go to Hyde Park to listen to the soap box speakers and enjoyed some of them tremendously. To me it was an interesting phase of the English political life of the street (I rarely listened to the religious speakers) and I was much amused by the tolerance of the "Bobbies" who would calmly endure the most rabid revolutionary speeches without turning a hair. Only once I heard one of them shout, " 'Ere, 'ere, stop that!" when an enthusiastic communist haranguer overstepped the legitimate boundaries of Red propaganda.

One day I met at my sister's Stephen Graham, the well known writer. He had visited Olga at her country place in the government of Orel during the war and altogether knew Russia quite well. He invited me to lunch in the old Cheshire Cheese and afterwards we sat and talked about Russia for a long while. That afternoon was certainly one of the nicest that I spent in London.

As I have said before one of my greatest pleasures was to go sight-seeing all by myself and to absorb all the English atmosphere that I possibly could. When spring came, the typical English spring, with its riot of bluebells and daffodils, I abandoned the museums and churches and other places of interest in town and turned towards the country. Richmond, Kew Gardens, Hampton Court, Windsor, Maidenhead—I went everywhere, usually on top of the bus, from which I walked in all directions. Golder's Green with its blossoming trees was at its very best then too and even the subways became unusually attractive with their great posters vividly portraying the flowers in season.

But though I enjoyed tremendously that sight-seeing period, on the other hand my financial worries had once more returned and were spoiling all my pleasure. On the nineteenth of May I wrote in my diary:

"I am frightened, frightened. My money is giving out again, I have only three pounds left and I still cannot find any work. What am I to do?"

Two weeks later, as I was slowly walking home down Addison Way, thinking about my financial problems that had reached the point where all the money I had left was the sixpenny bit in my pocket, I saw, seated on the grass in front of the cottage I lived in, a man with four very small children. Coming nearer I could see that they were all very poorly clad, nearly in tatters, and that their faces bore the unmistakable signs of hunger. As I came up to the pitiful little group the man suddenly looked up at me and with stark misery in his eyes but without saying a word, held out his hand. In that brief second a whole gamut of emotion passed over his face: entreaty, apology, despair and cowering shame.

"Are these your children?" I asked, my heart aching with pity as I read his feelings that I understood only too well, for had I not experienced them all?

"Yes, they're mine," he answered in a low well-bred voice.

"And your wife?"

"Dead," he whispered, and looking away from me dropped his hand.

That final gesture of utter despair decided me and in that moment I suddenly felt like a gambler. "If there is a Power above us," I thought, "it will take care of me right now, this very evening, if I give this man my last sixpence." And without another word I dropped the coin on the grass next to him and ran into the cottage.

"God bless you, lady," I heard him cry, and peeping through the window I saw him smile a kindly, honest smile, and then I knew that I had done right.

All that evening I sat in my room feverishly waiting for something to happen. At ten o'clock, just as my exultation was beginning to pass and I was going to bed, my landlady knocked on my door.

"Some one left this for you to-day when you were out," she said, "and then I forgot to give it to you when you returned," and handed me a sealed envelope. Tearing it open with trembling fingers I read the following words written by Mrs. Straker, an American friend of mine: "Your fan was sold yesterday for ten pounds and I am enclosing a check for it."

And thus I had a positive proof that even in these days miracles do happen.

In the beginning of June 1923 the course of my existence changed completely and irrevocably. It happened this way. One evening I was sitting in my sister's parlor reading when all of a sudden my brother-in-law looked up from his book and, apropos of nothing, said:

"An American woman came to-day to my office" (he was then working in the former Russian Consulate that had organized a sort of labor bureau which was trying to find work for the unemployed Russians), "and she asked if I knew of any Russian woman, young and of good family, she said, who would be willing to go with her to America to teach her French."

"Where does she live over there? What does she look like? What is her name? What hotel is she staying in here?" I asked, a sudden thought flashing through my mind.

"Well," he replied laughing, "that's a lot of questions to be answered. Let me see; she lives in a small town in the Middle West of America; she is quite elderly, and not good-looking, but dresses very smartly and youthfully; her name is Mrs. Hipper and she is staying at the Savoy. But why this sudden interest? Would you care to apply for the position?"

But I had been so often disappointed in my numerous quests for work that I didn't answer anything and kept my thoughts to myself. Next day however I put on my brown coat and bonnet-shaped hat (that I had bought with the first money I earned) and set forth to the Savoy Hotel. There I asked at the desk for Mrs. Hipper and being told that she had just been seen in the lobby, had her paged. As the boy went along calling her name loudly I gazed at the numerous women milling around and tried to guess which was Mrs. Hipper.

"I do hope it isn't that one," I prayed silently, seeing one that particularly did not appeal to me. She was an elderly person with reddish hair, nearsighted eyes protected by glasses, a mottled complexion and a most peevish unpleasant expression, as though she had just smelled something nasty and couldn't get rid of the odor. She was dressed very stylishly and wore many jewels. Suddenly as the boy passed her, calling out the name I had asked him to——she turned towards him and said something. My heart sank. The next minute the boy had returned and telling me to follow him led me up to the woman I was seeking.

"Well," she said, wrinkling up her nose and looking more discouraging than ever, "who are you and what do you want?"

I named myself explaining that I was the sister-in-law of Count B. whom she had spoken to about finding a Russian who would teach her French, and said that I would like to apply for the position and talk matters over with her.

"Very well," she said, snuffily as though she had a bad cold, "if Count B. sent you I suppose you're all right. You may come and see me to-morrow morning at ten o'clock in my suite here. Now I am busy and have no time to spare," and turning her back on me without so much as a parting nod she walked away in the opposite direction.

With flaming cheeks and beating heart I rushed out of the Savoy, firmly determined not to return the next morning. But when it arrived and I was feeling calmer and more philosophical I put on my hat and coat and once more started back to the hotel. Promptly at ten o'clock I was there and asked to be announced to Mrs. Hipper. The answer came that I was to wait until sent for. A quarter past ten, half past ten, a quarter to eleven, eleven—no message for me. My cheeks were burning again, my heart was thumping so loudly that I could hear it, my hands were cold and clammy and my throat felt tight and sore. Finally at ten minutes past eleven I was summoned upstairs and introduced into Mrs. Hipper's drawing-room. She was reading a letter as she reclined on the sofa, dressed in a bright pink tea gown covered with jewels. She barely glanced in my direction when I came in.

"Just a minute," she said as snuffily as the day before, and without asking me to sit down or even saying "how do you do."

Defiantly I looked around for a chair but every single one was covered with numerous parcels of all shapes and sizes and I realized that there was positively nothing for me to sit on except the floor. As I stood by the door wishing desperately that I could tell her what I thought of her manners and then walk out of the room, she suddenly turned towards me.

"Well, what are you standing there for?" she asked petulantly. "Come over here to the foot of the sofa where I can see you. And first of all show me your references."

I stared at her in incredulous amazement.

"My references," I gasped horrified; then remembering that this after all was a business talk I controlled myself and in a tone of voice that I hoped sounded impersonal and business like, continued: "Oh, yes; first of all there is my brother-in-law Count B., whom you talked to, and the Russian Consul General Mr. Onou, and Lord and Lady Carnock, and the Grand Duchess Xenia, and the Dowager Empress of Russia and many Americans whom I know, you can ask them all about me."

"All right, I will," she replied, looking at her pink nails, and then probably thinking that I was fibbing or making fun of her added haughtily, "and my reference is President Harding! I hope that will suit you. And now you may go, but first write down all those names and if the answers are satisfactory I will get in touch with you. By the way, if I hire you your salary will be a hundred dollars a month and you won't eat with the servants."

"But I don't want to come to you, not for anything

in the world," I cried indignantly, thoroughly roused by her last words, and turning away from her with head high up in the air walked out of her room. All that day I was positively ill from the treatment I had received and wishing to forget it went to Kew Gardens and sat for hours beneath a huge flowering bush.

Several days passed and I was beginning to forget the horrid incident when one evening I received a note saying:

"Dear Countess, I hope you will reconsider your decision and come to see me again. I think we can offer you one hundred and fifty dollars a month.

"Sincerely yours,
"Bella Hipper."

Her letter arrived at the psychological moment for that very day something painful happened that made me want desperately to earn some money regularly. So putting my pride in my pocket and my hat on my head, for the third time in ten days I started for the Savoy Hotel. This time I was received without any delay and was even greeted by a snuffy Hipper "good morning" when I came into her room. Then before anything further could be said Mr. Hipper arrived and from then on took entire charge of the proceedings. Right away he made a favorable impression on me and pleased me much more than his wife had. First of all he offered me a chair and made a few appropriate remarks about the weather. Then he spoke about America saying that no other country could compare to it, enthusiastically described his own home town in the Middle West and finally came to the point.

"We have interviewed several other Russians including Princess T., but Mrs. Hipper thinks that you'll do best. If you are willing to come we shall give you one hundred and twenty-five dollars a month, pay your traveling expenses and find you a decent room to live in not far from our house. As for your meals you will positively not eat with the servants."

My first impulse was to burst out laughing, it all seemed so queer and funny, but then remembering how hard it was to find any work in England and my imperative need of earning enough money each month to support myself decently without having to wonder where the next pennies would come from, I decided to accept his offer. As soon as I said that I would, he jumped up and shook hands with me, shouting warmly: "That's fine, glad to have you with us, I'm sure!" and even slapped me on the back while Mrs. Hipper looked on in cold disapproval.

"That's all right, Hiram, you don't have to get all excited about it and carry on this way," she remarked peevishly, again making one of her special faces, while two bright spots appeared on each cheek. "Leave Ma-

dame (for of course we'll call you Madame, not
Countess) alone with me now and I'll see you later."
Whereupon Mr. Hipper shook my hand once more saying somewhat ruefully: "Well, I guess I gotta be going. Good-by and good luck to you, Countess—Madame, I mean," and with a smile and plenty of friendly
nods left the room.

"Now, Madame," began Mrs. Hipper, "I wish you
to understand clearly your position. First of all I don't
want it known back home that you have a title, so you
will always be called Madame. Then you will not live
in the house but, as Mr. Hipper said, we'll find you a
room in town and a place to eat too. Breakfast however
you will have with the children. We have two adopted
little girls and I want them to learn French too, so at
breakfast time you will speak French to them. Of
course their nurse will eat with you, she's a nice girl
and will be good company for you. Then after breakfast you'll come to my drawing-room and teach me
French. I shall take you along with me driving and
marketing so as to speak French as much as possible. At
noon time you will have one hour for lunch and then
you will resume your duties with me until I see fit to
let you go home. Oh, yes, and I don't think that any
conversation with Mr. Hipper except 'bongjur and
bongsuar, monsur' will be necessary. Your dealings will
be entirely with me. And now good-by, I shall let you

know when your presence is needed for the final arrangements," whereupon she picked up a newspaper while I in a daze walked out of the room.

A few days later I received another note from her asking me to be at the Savoy the next morning in order to go with her and Mr. Hipper to the American Consul General. As I came into the lobby I found them both waiting for me and without further delay we started for the Consulate. There we were received by the Consul General, an exceedingly courteous and charming man whom I had met before at the homes of my American friends. He seemed a trifle surprised to hear of my intention of going for a year to the Midwestern home of the Hippers and said that as the Russian quota for teachers was full for the time being I could not possibly sail next week with my employers on the *Mauretania*.

"But," suggested Mrs. Hipper, "if she cannot pass in her capacity of teacher maybe she could pass as our maid or cook."

I nearly fell off my chair, protesting vehemently that I could not even fry an egg properly and that if the immigration authorities became suspicious of me and ordered me to cook a dinner at Ellis Island I wouldn't know what to do! At that the Consul burst out laughing, then quickly regaining his seriousness turned towards the Hippers.

"Of course that is out of the question! How could

you even suggest such a thing? Besides being illegal it would be unfair to put the Countess in such a position. No, I'm sorry to say she cannot sail until the 23rd of June and when she does, she goes in the capacity of teacher and no other."

Then it was decided that the Hippers would leave as arranged on the *Mauretania* while I would follow two weeks later on the first available ship that sailed on the 23rd. That settled, various formalities had to be gone through, and then I departed shaking hands warmly with the Consul General and gratefully thanking him for his courteousness and kindness towards me.

IV

ALL my American friends were anxious to hear the
outcome of my final interview with the Hippers and Mrs. Straker immediately said that
she would go to see them and offer to take charge of all
the necessary arrangements for my departure. In two
days she arrived triumphantly at my room and announced that my employers had given her two hundred
dollars with which she was to pay for my journey and
also half of my month's salary in advance so that I
could buy myself a few new clothes. After that my life
became a whirl. First of all Mrs. Straker went to the
Cunard booking offices and secured a stateroom for me
on the *Franconia* that was sailing on the 23rd of June
on her maiden voyage. And when I opened my eyes

wide and gasped: "What—a whole state-room for me alone, Mrs. Straker? But is that necessary?" she answered emphatically, "Most decidedly *yes*, you know you've got to go in the right way!" Whereupon I threw my arms around her and hugged her as hard as I could.

The next thing then was to buy a few clothes which I did at the dressmaking establishment of a Russian friend of mine, Madam Volkoff. A gray knitted traveling suit with a gray silk jumper to match,—a white muslin afternoon frock embroidered with gold brown flowers and a very plain black silk evening dress that fitted me to perfection—these were the dresses I bought. Then I got a gray silk hat with blue ribbons, gray suède shoes and a pair of black satin ones, stockings and some necessary articles of underwear. I couldn't afford to buy a new traveling coat and had to be content with the funny shaped brown one that made me look like a table hand bell when I had it on.

Then I had to go around bidding my friends good-by, which took quite a lot of time as they all had something particular to say about America, whether they had been there or not, and plenty of instructions and advice. Finally the great day dawned and when my brief and easy packing was over, at eleven o'clock in the morning, I left Golder's Green for Euston station accompanied by my sister, her husband and her son. At the station I found Sofia Dmitrievna Evreinova, who together with a few other friends had kindly come to see me off. Then at eleven fifty my train started and the great adventure, my journey to America, began, while once more I waved good-by to the small group on the platform, just as I had done eight months before at the Baltic station when I left Petrograd and Russia to become a wandering exile. Feeling pretty miserable and lonesome I soon turned to my panacea of all woes— the Diary, and this is what I wrote then:

Saturday, 23rd of June, 1923

"God bless me! A new chapter of my life has just begun: I am on my way to America. I am alone in the compartment and therefore have been crying comfortably in the proper fashion without interruption. Now I cannot cry any more, so I write instead. I feel very sleepy, crying always affects me that way, but I won't allow myself to sleep as I want to look out of the window and see this part of England. So far it's all alike: rolling hills, narrow streams, pastures, fields and small red brick cottages with lots of flowers around them. Again I'm thinking of Nana and again I'm beginning to cry. What would she say if she knew that her Dickey Bird was going as a teacher to a small American town where she doesn't know a single cat. For some reason instead of going down my cheeks in the usual way the tears are running towards the end of my nose and from there, becoming one great big drop, splash onto my paper in the most dismal fashion. . . .

"Now we're in Liverpool and the train is wending its way towards the dock where the *Franconia* is moored. "Wending its way" is the correct description of the progress of this train for it barely advances at a snail-like pace, as though it were cautiously feeling its way over the squeaking rails. In front of the engine a man is actually walking! We pass enormous warehouses that smell of leather, tar and mice. It has taken us exactly fifteen minutes to crawl up to the dock. Now at last we're stopping, and a porter has jumped in, grabbed my things and mysteriously disappeared with them. How on earth am I to find them?"

An hour later on board the Franconia

"Well, I climbed off the train and walked towards the *Franconia,* but couldn't get on her for quite a while on account of crowds of visitors that had come to see the new ship before she started on her maiden voyage. At last with the help of an official I got on board and was taken to my cabin, B. 34. It's beautiful, really and truly! There are two berths in it and everything looks so new and shiny and smells so clean of fresh paint. Next door there is a bath-room—my very own private one too. Finding my luggage in the cabin I immediately unpacked my Holy Icons, photographs and books and

arranged them on the tables making the place look
home-like and cozy. It's the very nicest room I've had
for years and I'm delighted with it. I was so busy un-
packing that I never even noticed when the ship got
under way and only realized that when I came on deck
and saw that we were about three miles out of Liverpool. At first the view was not particularly attractive but
now it has become beautiful in a severe, rugged way as
we pass the coast of Wales with its high cliffs. I just
walked around the deck and from the other side could
see only a boundless expanse of sea. Night has fallen, a
clear luminous summer night and the moon is playing
hide and seek among the clouds. For some reason I
think of Longfellow's 'Ballad of Carmilhan' (the
Musician's tale of the Wayside Inn)—one of the favorite poems of my childhood that Olga used often to
recite to me. The minute she began: 'At Stralsund on
the Baltic Sea . . .' I would become silent and in
speechless terror listen to the gruesome tale about
'Klaboterman the Kobold of the Sea' and shriek pierc-
ingly when she reached the words:

> *'Them to torment was his delight*
> *And worry them by day and night*
> *And pinch them black and blue,'*

which she would obligingly illustrate with a few colorful pinches on my small body. 'Perhaps we'll see the

specter ship,' I think, peering anxiously out to sea, now flooded with ghostly moonlight. But that thought incredibly makes me shiver in the way I used to long ago, and to forget it I'm going to stop writing now and shall run back to my cheerful cabin."

Same evening

"I'm in my berth now, luxuriously writing by the light of a regular reading lamp. Such comfort! The whole evening has been unusually nice and I am still chuckling delightedly over it. It was fun to get ready for dinner and bathe in that lovely bathroom and dress in the right kind of a frock and see how nice I looked in the long mirror. Then the excellent dinner properly served at a well-appointed table and tasting ever so good, the music, the nice-looking people and the wonderful moonlit evening on deck! For years and years I haven't experienced anything like it and can hardly realize that it isn't all a dream. My berth is so soft and comfortable too, like a cradle, and the slight movement of the ship is ever so soothing. It's all too good to be true."

Sunday, June 24th

"I slept and slept and slept last night as I haven't slept for ages, a wonderful, dreamless unbroken sleep until nine o'clock this morning. At 10 I had breakfast downstairs and just now am sitting on deck gazing at

[118]

'Queenstown,' for we're actually in Ireland and I've missed many sights thanks to my endless slumbers. I heard some one say that there was a time this morning when both shores could be seen, that of England and Ireland, and am wondering if that can be true. Many new passengers have come aboard and the ship is on its way once more. A woman is screaming that she wants to be put ashore immediately, as she did not know that this was the *Franconia's* maiden voyage and, that being the case, refuses flatly to continue such a risky journey. One of the ship's officers is arguing with her and at the same time gently leading her away somewhere inside. An amused crowd is following them, but I feel too comfortable and happy in my deck chair to move."

Later

"Since we left the Bay it seems to me that we have been passing the shores of Ireland for hours. I never realized before how vast Ireland is, having always thought of her as being 'just an Island.' Now I see that she is really a small continent and am respectfully impressed. And another thing too—she certainly deserves her poetic name 'The Emerald Isle,' for she is as vividly green as central Russia in spring.

"Then I did some exploring on board and discovered the great swimming pool, the gymnasium with all its cunning contraptions—such as an electric boat where one learns to row, electric horses, bicycles and so forth. It's all very amusing but a trifle sickening as all those things rock making me think of an amusement park. I go up on deck again and find that we are in the open sea now, with the shore of Ireland barely visible on the horizon. I am sitting in my deck chair writing this; later I shall read."

And so the hours of the first day flowed gently and pleasantly on.

Soon I became acquainted with my deck chair neighbors; to my right Mr. and Mrs. William E. Clarke, to my left Mr. and Mrs. Frederick T. Vaux—both elderly couples from Chicago. Then I met a young English couple, the Cyril Murrays, and their friend, a bachelor called Mr. Young, and Doctor Maitland, the ship's surgeon who bore a striking resemblance to the actor Milton Sills. They were all very nice people and we soon formed quite a friendly little group. The peace and quiet of my life on board, the beautiful weather, the comfort of my cabin, the excellent meals, the pleasant companionship of my new acquaintances—all contributed to make my days perfectly happy. It was like a lull in my stormy existence and for the first time in years I felt rested and at peace with the whole world. I forgot that I was a homeless penniless exile, that I had been battered by years of suffering and was bound for an unknown destination. I lived in the present, from day to day, utterly oblivious of the past and the future, fiercely enjoying every minute of pleasure and comfort, on a footing of equality with everybody else. My cabin was my home, just the same as for other passengers; I ate the same food they did, had a deck chair like theirs; bathed in the swimming pool, played squash racquets, chatted, laughed and danced. Though I had only three dresses, still I was decently clad and looked just as well groomed as the other women. In every way my life was no different from the lives of my fellow passengers. Everything was paid for and I had no worries, not a care in the world that week. No one knew how poor I was, nor that I was on my way to teach French in a small Middle Western town where I would live in a room in a boarding house and "not eat with the servants,"—therefore no one condescended to me, no one pitied me, no one was sorry for my plight. It was such a relief to live the life that everybody else did and I shall always remember that lull in my existence with gratitude and a sigh of regret that it passed so quickly away. I could have stayed on that ship forever as I would on a magic island, with the horrors of the past forgotten, and the pain of the future unknown.

The last evening on board, when we were anchored in New York Harbor for the night, I went all over the ship saying good-by to her as I would to an old friend.

For the first time since I sailed I could not sleep and sat up late on deck fully realizing that the "lull" was over and that next morning I had to face the grim realities of life once more. Somewhere in the distance I could hear the popular strains of "Mr. Gallagher and Mr. Shean" that I had heard for the first time on board and that, therefore, would always remind me of my first crossing. The absurd words that had always amused me so much suddenly sounded sad, even tragic, and with a little stab of pain I found myself joining the far away chorus, that was somewhere across the water, improvising my own words and singing, "Is it finished, Mr. Gallagher? Absolutely, Mr. Shean."

"Why, what's the matter?" I heard two concerned voices ask me and looking up saw the Murrays gazing at me worriedly. "We heard you singing softly but your voice sounded so sad, even though you were singing that ridiculous song, that we simply had to come out and see what had happened. And you look sad too," they continued, sitting down on either side of me and peering anxiously at my face.

"What is the matter?" repeated the little woman, patting my hand while her husband, evidently wishing to cheer me up, laughingly shouted: "Well, whatever it is it's not very serious! Imagine any one feeling badly over Mr. Gallagher and Mr. Shean, for that's what you were doing! really and truly!"

And he was right; that was just what I was doing, nearly weeping over Mr. Gallagher and Mr. Shean. Strangely enough that song became part of my collection of tunes that are in some way connected with various periods of my life and whenever I hear it, to this day, it hurts a little and brings back so vividly that last evening on board the *Franconia*.

Next morning, July 3rd, I went through all the necessary formalities that await incoming foreigners and then, having packed my belongings in my two little suitcases, went on deck. Here to my astonishment I was suddenly surrounded by a group of unknown young men whom I most decidedly had not seen on board before and who without any preliminaries began to fire at me a lot of amazing questions.

"What is your exact name?"

"How do you spell it?"

"How old are you?"

"Were you ever married?"

"Have you any children?"

"Why did you come to the United States?"

"What do you think of our country?"

"How long are you going to stay?"

"Whom are you going to visit?" and so forth, at the same time whipping out of their pockets little writing pads and evidently preparing themselves to write down my answers.

"But who are you?" I managed at last to stammer idiotically, completely bewildered and wondering who on earth they were.

"We? Oh, we're the Press, don't you know that?" they answered, grinning widely at my stupidity. "Why, haven't you any reporters on the other side?"

"Reporters, oh, that's who you are!" I gasped, now thoroughly frightened, for in London before I sailed I had been told a great deal about the terrifying on-slaughts of American reporters and warned that they would ply me with questions in order to make a "good story" out of me. How could I have forgotten those friendly warnings and why had I come on deck? Wildly I looked around hoping to escape, but there was not the slightest chance of doing so, for I was firmly surrounded by a circle of smiling but very decided-looking young men, who clearly had no intention of letting me run away. Desperately I looked at them and then suddenly, surprisingly . . . liked them! They seemed so jolly and yet at the same time so painstakingly earnest, as if their lives depended on getting some kind of an answer out of me. And though they were all grinning good-naturedly, the expression in their eyes was intent and serious and tremendously alert.

"All right," I said, beginning to grin too, "all right, I'll tell you how old I am and how to spell my name and all that, but let's go where everybody won't be staring at us and where we can talk in peace."

"Say, that's mighty decent of you," one of them exclaimed approvingly, while another one hurriedly led the way to the deserted lounge.

"Now," they said in one breath when we got there and sat down in a circle, "now!" and then my first American interview began. They were really very nice about it all, and when the next day I read a number of pleasant little stories about myself, I decided once for all that I positively liked reporters and would never be afraid of them again.

When at last they left me with friendly little nods and grins, I went on deck again and joining the small group of people that I knew, watched the great sky line of New York loom nearer and nearer as our ship slowly approached the dock. And as I gazed spell-bound at that stupendous mass of buildings and towers, wondering why I felt that I had seen it before,—I suddenly remembered with a start a strange thing that happened to me a few weeks ago in London, before I ever knew that I was coming to America.

I was going to lunch that day with Lady Carnock at one o'clock and was walking from the subway towards her house in Cadogan Gardens, when, glancing at my wrist watch, I realized that I would arrive there too early and decided to walk around for half an hour. As

I slowly went along, gazing into shop windows to pass the time, I came to a jeweler's and mechanically stopped to look at his display. But curiously enough his window was empty, save for a fair-sized crystal, mounted on a stand of thin golden wire beneath which rippled the folds of a large piece of white velvet. It was one of those crystals that one always pictures soothsayers gazing into, but was unusually lovely as it caught the rays of the sun and glittered like an enormous diamond or like a globe of ice in a field of snow. Fascinated I stared at it, watching the shafts of light strike it, and then dartingly rebound in multicolored pin-points of flame. Then all of a sudden, a cloud passed over the sun, the fire died out of the crystal and it became dull and gray. Disappointed that the lovely play of light had ended so soon, I was about to move away when, glancing at the crystal once more, I noticed with surprise that it was no longer dull and gray but had changed again and, though not sparkling and shining as at first, now had strange, moving streaks of color in it that seemed to be forming patterns and taking on definite shapes. Bending down eagerly, with my face pressed against the great window pane, I then saw that the movement of those streaks of color had stopped and that a definite picture, somewhat like a mirage, had come to life in the crystal. A wide expanse of bluish gray, like water, occupied the foreground of that strange little mirage, while back of it stood out clearly the outline of a great power-ful city, fantastic and unreal to my Russian eyes. Hardly daring to breathe for fear of breaking the spell, I gazed, while for a brief space of time the picture stood out clear and still. Then the sun broke out again and the crystal became once more a ball of fire. Trembling with excitement I rushed back to Cadogan Gardens and, ar-riving fifteen minutes late for lunch, breathlessly told Lady Carnock about my strange experience. She laughed kindly, calling me an incorrigible little dreamer and said she wished she could believe in fairy magic too. But though I had to come back to real life during lunch and talk and act as though nothing unusual had happened, all that day I could not forget the crystal and the fan-tastic picture that I had seen in it. Then with the ex-citement of getting ready to go to America, it gradually faded away out of my memory until the morning of my arrival in New York, when from the deck of the *Fran-conia* I saw the outline of a strange-looking gigantic city and realized with a shock that it was the very same out-line that I had seen in my magic crystal.

"You are very pale, are you feeling well?" asked Mrs. Clarke, who was standing by me.

"It's the excitement of seeing New York for the first time that makes her pale," said her husband jovially. "And no wonder; it's a great sight, the finest in the world to my eyes," he continued, offering me his binoc-

ulars so that I could see the slowly approaching buildings in detail. I didn't answer, wishing again that I could
get away from everybody and be alone for a while, but
I was tightly jammed in on three sides by the crowds of
passengers who had all come to look at New York and I
was obliged to remain standing in my place by the railing.

But as usual in that first year after leaving Russia,
when I cried so often and so easily, the tears began to
run down my cheeks faster than I could wipe them off.

"Don't cry, Countess, don't cry, it's all right," murmured a man next to me who had been staring at me intently for quite a long while, and whom suddenly I
recognized to be one of the reporters that had questioned
me half an hour ago. "Don't cry," he repeated, adding
soothingly: "I know it's all new and kind of strange to
you and you're home-sick and all that, but you'll like
it when you get there; they all do!"

Little did I guess that next morning I would read in
one of the newspapers the following words, written undoubtedly by the sympathetic reporter.

"Maid of Honor to Empress, fortune gone, arrives
in U. S. like Immigrant."

"A lonely young woman dressed in gray leaned over
the rail of the steamer *Franconia* as that vessel came
into New York Harbor from Liverpool to-day. As the
ship neared the pier the young woman hid her face in
her hands and wept. She was the Countess Irina W.

Keller, once Maid of Honor to the Empress Alexandra of Russia. She was a long way from home and homesick."

At last the *Franconia* docked and bidding all my new friends farewell I went ashore where I was instantly taken to my letter K. in the Customs, closely followed by the reporters who seemed to be much interested in my luggage.

"Is that all you've got?" asked one of them, pointing incredulously to my two little suitcases.

"Why, yes, that's all," I answered, wishing that I had at least one trunk that I could boastfully call my own.

"Well, well," was all they said, looking at each other significantly when my suitcases were opened and their contents divulged and "well, well!" again when a little osprey feather came fluttering out from between the folds of my dress. That feather had been given to me just before I left London and was one of my prize possessions.

"Ospreys are not permitted to enter the States," said the inspector severely, picking up the offending feather and angrily putting it back in my suitcase that he then closed with a slam.

"Oh, I'm sorry, I didn't know," I said nervously, fingering my thin purse and, as misfortunes always will happen in a row, at the same time bursting open my glove at the end of my right forefinger.

"Hum," said the inspector, looking at my glove, then at my purse, then at my suitcases again. "Hum" . . . then "that's all, you may go," he growled, turning away from me while a reporter shouted something mysterious that sounded to me like "adaboy."

"Adaboy, what's that?" I asked, but before he could answer a short fat red-faced individual came tearing along towards me, mopping his forehead and excitedly waving a letter.

"My name is Mr. Midstream and are you the Countess Keller?" he cried, rushing up to me and thrusting the letter under my very nose. "Because if you are, then read this!" Whereupon I read the following words which my friends the reporters read too as they peered over my shoulder:

"Dear John," it said. "Will you do me a favor and meet at the dock Countess K. who is arriving on the *Franconia* July 3rd. Take her to lunch and then put her on a train to Metropole. Tell her then to change trains and take one to Dawn. There's no use putting her on a fast train because of the extra fare involved so put her on a slow one. For whatever you spend on her send me an itemized bill and I will reimburse you at once."

> "Sincerely yours,
> "Hiram Hipper."

As though I had just received a slap in the face I stared stupidly at the words: "No use putting her on a fast train because of the extra fare involved," while the reporters whistled softly behind me.

"Say, who's the big-hearted guy that wrote this swell letter?" asked one of them in a tone of voice that sounded to me rather ironical.

"Guy?" I repeated, perplexed, "Guy? no, that isn't his name, it's Hiram——" but before I could say it Mr. Midstream interrupted me, angrily shouting:

"None of their damn business, lady! Come on, we've no time to lose . . . As for you," he turned towards the reporters, "beat it, understand me? Beat it!"

"Beat what?" I cried anxiously, now completely bewildered, and wondering what the man was talking about, but without further explanations he caught my arm with one hand while he waved the other angrily at the reporters, making clucking noises at them as though he were shooing chickens away.

There they stood, a group of impudent-looking, grinning young men, with hats pushed back on their heads and hands in their pockets, but I liked them and trusted them and suddenly felt that I was leaving old friends behind me to follow an unknown man.

"Good-by," I cried, looking over my shoulder once more as Mr. Midstream hurried me away.

"Not yet good-by, we'll see you at the station," they

shouted back, and for some reason that answer cheered me up considerably.

As soon as we reached the street I was put in a taxi and off we went to the Pennsylvania Hotel, "where I'll *buy you* a lunch," as Mr. Midstream obligingly explained. At the hotel we went straight to the dining room and there my escort ordered the strangest lunch I had ever eaten: clams to begin with,—then a fruit salad and pumpkin pie for dessert. I gingerly swallowed a clam, but it made me feel sick; got a shock when I found that my salad was sweet, and nearly choked over a mouthful of the strange pie. Then the orchestra, that up to that time had been playing cheerful things, started Madam Butterfly's death song which evidently was the last straw as far as I was concerned, for I burst into tears and burying my face in my napkin wept bitterly.

"Oh, Countess, what is the matter? Don't you like your lunch? Are you too hot? Oh, what is it?" cried Mr. Midstream, jumping up and fluttering around me wildly as he waved his napkin over my head to refresh me. But I couldn't say a word and probably seeing every one in the room stare at us, he rapidly paid the bill and rushed me out of the hotel back into a taxi again.

"A ride is what you need to buck you up," he said optimistically as we tore down the street, stopping so suddenly that I bumped my head painfully and then laughed a little as I remembered the poem that my brother had invented and written in my autograph album when I was small:

I shall write into your album
Bump your head against the wall
Then you'll suddenly remember
That you're beloved by all.

"There you see," said Mr. Midstream cheerfully, "didn't I tell you that you'd feel better? Now this is Fifth Avenue—the finest street in the world, my girl, don't you ever forget that!"

I looked out of the window and was disappointed. Somehow I had expected Fifth Avenue to be like the outline of New York that I had seen from the ship,—as fantastic and unreal as anything I had ever seen before. But this was just an ordinary street, wide and handsome, true, that might have belonged to any large city.

"Oh, but I thought that your buildings were entirely made of polished steel and shining white bricks," I said with such apparent disappointment in my voice that Mr. Midstream gazed at me reprovingly.

"First time I've heard any one say they didn't think Fifth Avenue the finest street in the world," he declared, and then evidently having had enough of my company, ordered the taxi driver to take us to the station.

[133]

"I guess it's about time for you to be going soon," he said hopefully, and I passively agreed.

At the station he bought me ten cents' worth of candy and a newspaper while I stood by wondering if he'd put them down on "Hiram's itemized bill." Then, just as we were about to go to the train my reporters came dashing along still grinning and with their hats still on the backs of their heads.

"Oh, there you are at last," I cried delightedly. "I was afraid you'd be late!"

"Don't worry, we're never late anywhere," they answered cheerfully, then turning towards Mr. Midstream shouted: "Well, here we are again, you old . . ." I don't remember exactly whether they said gorilla or chimpanzee or what, anyhow what they called him had to do with the monkey family.

"Come on, come on!" exclaimed Mr. Midstream testily, grabbing my arm once more and running me towards the train.

"Good-by, Countess, good luck!" shouted the reporters. "And oh, say, mister, we've got the name of your spendthrift friend Hiram all right, and we'll print it in full, never fear!"

Grumbling all kinds of things about them, Mr. Midstream finally got me on the train and in a few minutes it started me towards my destination—the small town of Dawn in the Middle West.

V

A T first I sat in my corner with closed eyes, bewildered and exhausted, then having rested a
little, began to look around. My first impression of a Pullman car had been formed long ago, when
as a child I used to look through my stereoscope at a
favorite picture representing the interior of an American Pullman with passengers dressed in the fashionable
attire of the gay nineties all smiling pleasantly at each
other. According to the picture I was in the wrong place,
and a debonair, bewhiskered man in a straw hat and
checked suit should have been in it, smiling condescend-
ingly and protectively bending from his waist in the direction of a fascinating young woman, with puffed
sleeves and an enormous hat, who sat next to him with

a coy look in her eyes. Then opposite, there should have been two serious-looking, money-making men reading their newspapers and thinking only of their millions, while in the aisle itself small children disported themselves gayly. But the real picture was quite different: next to me was a little old lady with snow-white hair and a kind, comfortable look about her, opposite sat a young couple that certainly did not smile pleasantly at each other or at anybody else, and the aisle was empty. Infinitely preferring the Pullman of the stereoscope to the actual one, I closed my eyes again and went back to my childhood. That stereoscope, I pondered, must have been of American make, for now that I came to think of it, its pictures were all connected with American life. There was one that I liked particularly too, that showed a high mountain called Pike's Peak on top of which, on the very brink of a terrific precipice, stood a brave but reckless man on one leg, his other one perilously raised above the edge of the chasm. "One step forward and he plunges to his death," the caption read beneath that alarming picture, that always caused my heart to flutter and chased little shivers of ecstatic fright down my spine. "One step forward . . ." I'd murmur to myself admiringly and wonder if all Americans were as brave as that man.

Then there was the picture of Uncle Sam attired in his striped suit and tall hat which I thought was the

American national costume and firmly believed that all American men dressed that way. In fact, whenever I heard the words "American Man" I instantly visualized Uncle Sam with his goatee, striped suit and high hat, and even to this day when I say "I am married to an American"—the picture that always flashes first like lightning through my mind is that of my husband with a goatee (which he really doesn't have) and dressed in his national costume. Besides being so educational, that stereoscope was a source of constant pleasure to me and I loved it dearly too. It had a peculiar odor all of its own and smelled intriguingly of wood and glue and something else that I could not define but that was most pleasing to my nostrils. Then it had a velvet rim that ran along its edges and felt so soft and nice against my forehead and cheeks. Altogether it was a very delightful thing and one of the prize possessions of my playroom.

Our train being a slow one, that probably would have won the approval of even Mr. Hipper, stopped frequently and I could not understand why at all the stations there was the constant noise of firing and crackling. At last unable to conceal my inquisitiveness any longer I turned towards the old lady next to me and asked her what all that firing meant.

"Oh, don't you know it's the Fourth of July to-day, Independence Day, and everybody—that is, mostly all our small boys—tries to make as much noise as possible," she obligingly replied, and then with a twinkle in her eye added: "But you must be a foreigner not to know that. English, perhaps, or Scotch for you roll your r's and have a little burr in your speech, or maybe French." When I told her what my nationality was she seemed very much interested and soon we were discussing all the great problems of the world: war, revolution, socialism and even communism. She proved to be one of those delightful old ladies who are up to date in everything, read and study a great deal, travel and have very decided opinions on all subjects. Evidently understanding how forlorn and lonesome I felt, she sat up late talking to me and trying to cheer me as best she could. As she was getting off the train early next morning she bid me good-by when it was time for me to climb into my upper berth and putting her arm around my shoulders said gently:

"Now remember what I told you: it takes all kinds of people to make up a world, in America as well as anywhere else, and you must not judge us all by the various types that you may come into contact with at first. Life probably seems very perplexing and even terrifying to you right now, but don't forget the prophecy of an old woman who has had a great deal of experience— and that is: that everything will come out all right in the end. My name is Mrs. Crump and I am sure that we will meet again and that you will then tell me how

[138]

much you have grown to care for us and perhaps even never want to leave us any more."

I have always considered her comforting and prophetic words as my real welcome to America and do hope that some day I'll see her again and tell her that she was right.

My upper berth on a hot July night was anything but pleasant and as I turned and twisted and bumped myself on all sides, first trying to undress, then, that wild feat accomplished, doing my best to make myself comfortable—I muttered all kinds of nasty little things about the inefficiency and lack of comfort of American sleepers. I had always thought that they were the acme of ease and comfort and, as the truth dawned on me, I realized that that was my second disappointment that day, the first one being about the streets of New York that I had pictured lined entirely with shining skyscrapers made of glittering steel and snow-white bricks. Hotter and hotter became my berth, louder and louder sounded the great chorus of snores around me, while wherever we stopped, despite the lateness of the hour, the noise of crackling and firing and exploding doggedly persisted.

"That firing is my own private welcome to the United States," I thought, and then remembered another welcome ten years earlier, when my mother and I were sightseeing one morning in the town of Rostov the

Great. We had just arrived there by train and were passing through the streets in a drosky cab when my mother suddenly remarked whimsically:

"Do you know, Cherry Tree, that in the old days, when a Prince or Princess of Rostov came to the town— all the church bells in the Kremlin" (the town of Rostov the Great has one of the finest Kremlins in Russia) "used to ring out a veritable carillon of welcome. But here I am" (she was born Princess Lobanov of Rostov) "passing through the town where once in the Middle Ages the Princes of Rostov reigned—and not a single bell is welcoming us!"

Barely had she spoken when a tremendous peal of church bells suddenly burst forth over the town. Peal upon peal shook the air all around us like the waves of a sea of glorious sound, while I, in an ecstasy of delight lifted my arms high over my head with the sensation of a swimmer ready to dive.

"Oh, Muzzie," I gasped, turning towards her, but stopped short leaving my words unspoken, for she was sitting straight as an arrow in the shabby old cab, her head high up, her eyes shining and a rapt expression of happiness on her face.

Then, as suddenly as they had begun, the bells stopped and we stared at each other in awe. But as I belonged to a younger, more inquisitive and more irreverent generation I was the first to break the silence.

"Why did the church bells ring that way?" I asked the drosky driver shakily, still floating in my world of magic.

"Why?" he answered in a hoarse voice as he turned around on his seat and sent a whiff of alcoholic breath in our direction, "why . . . because it's Sunday to-day." That broke the spell and sent us off in gales of laughter. However that evening, as we were sitting on the deck of the steamer that was carrying us down the Volga to the Caspian Sea, looking at the moon and breathing in deeply the fragrance of new mown hay that the soft wind brought us from the shore, my mother dreamily said:

"Just the same the bells *did* ring and I had my welcome in Rostov."

That memory came back to me so clearly as I lay in my stuffy berth, that I sat up and, unable to bear it any longer, got up and went onto the platform of the car. There I stood for a long while and was still standing, when early in the morning we came to Mrs. Crump's station, and I saw her once more as she passed me on her way out.

"Good luck and au revoir," she cried, waving her hand when the train began to move, and I, with a sinking heart, watched her trim little figure soon disappear, thinking hopelessly that now I had lost my very last friend.

On and on we went through all that long, hot, dusty day, while I looked drearily out of the window at the endless sun-scorched plains of the Middle West. Time dragged terrifically and when at last we reached the great city of Metropole it seemed to me that I had been in that train for ages. No one met me at the station and remembering the instructions of Mr. Midstream I asked the porter to put me on the train for Dawn. He asked me whether I wanted a seat in a Pullman or in the coach, whereupon I, knowing from the past two days' experience what a Pullman was, and being utterly ignorant about coaches, except that I vaguely surmised that they were drawn by horses, promptly replied with the detached air of a veteran traveler: "Pullman, please." However my dismay cannot be described when, just as I had settled down comfortably, the conductor came along and after examining my ticket politely requested me to pay for my Pullman seat. Horrified, I stared at him in silence, knowing only too well that I had nothing but three cents left in my purse, while he stared back at me in surprise evidently wondering why I didn't produce the necessary sum. Red to the roots of my hair, I stammered:

"Oh, I'm so sorry, I didn't know, and I'm all out of money," while at the same time agonized visions of being put off the train raced through my mind. But the man didn't seem angry or upset at my information, and merely remarked as he threw his chewing gum out of the window:

"Then you'll have to move into the coach, ma'am," to my immense relief. Horses or no horses the coach suddenly appeared to me as a haven of safety where I would be allowed to continue my journey to Dawn, and I followed the man as he led the way with my suitcases, hardly noticing the amused stares of the other passengers.

VI

WHEN finally the train stopped in Dawn and I got off with my two suitcases I found myself forlornly standing on the platform not knowing what to do next. Again no one had come to meet me, no other passengers had got off the train, no porter was in view. After waiting vainly for some one to turn up or for something to happen I lifted my suitcases and trudged down the long platform towards the station. There wasn't any one there either except a woman behind the newspaper stand. I went up to her.

"Could you please tell me how to get to the Hiram Hipper residence?" I asked. She stared at me for a minute, then said sulkily, "Well, there are several ways: you can walk, or you can take the street car, or you can hire a taxi. Haven't you ever been here before?"

I shook my head silently and was about to turn away when suddenly she called me back in a very different tone of voice:

"Say, oh, say," she cried excitedly, "are you the new teacher that was to come all the way from France? The children's nurse, Anna, was telling me about you the other day and said that they were expecting you soon."

"Yes, I am the French teacher," I replied, the words somehow sticking in my throat as once more I lifted my suitcases and walked towards the door.

Outside there were no taxis in sight but soon one came tearing along and stopped right next to me while the driver shouted:

"You're the French teacher, aren't you? Miss Ball at the news stand called up and said you was lookin' for a taxi. And how's old Paree?" he added as I got in and he started to drive. "You see," he continued, "I was over there when the war was on and could speak French quite well. Hinkey Dinkey parley voo . . . commong sa va—venay eessee toot sweet . . . I haven't forgotten it yet, have I? And it's great to see a Frenchie again," he added, turning around and looking at me approvingly.

I couldn't help laughing! Here was my welcome to Dawn, original perhaps, but kind-hearted and sincere.

"And, say, Madmozel," he rattled on as we passed

through a crowded street and then came to a shady avenue, apparently the residential part of the town, "say, you're a lucky girl, you're goin' to live in a swell place! Why, the Hippers have the biggest house in town, a palace, I call it."

We drove up to a large, pretentious-looking square house with very small grounds around it, while on either side the smaller houses of the neighbors seemed dwarfed and humble. The taxi man then turned into a private driveway, stopped and shouting, "Here we are," opened the door and, taking my suitcases, led the way to a side porch.

"I brought you to the service entrance; that's all right, isn't it?" he asked, looking at me a trifle anxiously.

"Quite all right," I answered shakily, and then before he could ring the bell added:

"I'm sorry I have no money to pay you, but I'll ask some one here to do it for me, and thank you very much for your kind welcome, I'm glad that you like Paris, good-by."

"That's all right, don't worry! I'll charge it to old Hipper . . . bongsouar, adew, toot sweet," he cried, politely doffing his cap, and then the door opened and I entered my new home.

A number of people advanced to meet me and the next minute numerous handshakes greeted me on all sides. A tall girl, with a slightly supercilious look on her plain but clever face, began to introduce every one.

"This is Mr. Goodman, the butler," she said, "and this is Miss Mary, madam's own personal attendant, and Miss Kathleen, the parlor help, and Miss Minnie, the chef, and Miss Hilda, her assistant, and Mr. Brown, the chauffeur. And I am Miss Anna, the children's nurse, and one might say madam's companion too. And what is your name, please?"

"Oh, Mrs. Hipper said that she wished me to be called just madame," I answered, gravely shaking hands with all my new fellow workers, while Miss Anna went on hospitably:

"You see, Mr. and Mrs. Hipper have just gone out to play bridge and asked me to take charge of you. I hope you had a comfortable journey. We watched every day in the papers to see if your ship had sunk, icebergs, you know, at this time of the year."

"And how about a nice little supper?" interrupted Minnie, the cook, beaming at me, her fair hair wet and her wide pleasant face aglow from a very apparent recent contact with plenty of soap. "It won't take me but a minute to fix you something tasty. A few slices of cold ham, perhaps, and some lovely potato salad that we all had for supper, and a piece of my delicious cherry pie."

"Thank you, that will be very nice," I replied, wondering if I was going to eat in the kitchen after all. Kathleen, the little Irish parlor maid, had evidently the same thought for she inquired at once in her soft brogue: "And where shall I take her tray?"

"Oh!" exclaimed Anna, as though thunderstruck. "Oh, I never thought to ask Mrs. Hipper about that! Let me see: you couldn't eat in the big dining room because Mr. Goodman has just cleared away there and we couldn't mess up his table again. And you couldn't eat in our dining room for that same reason, and you wouldn't care to eat in the kitchen, would you?" she asked dubiously. "And it's too hot on the porch, besides, there are many flies there . . ."

"How about the drawing room or the library?" suggested Mary in a low and quiet voice as though she hadn't much strength left in her very thin, genteel-looking body.

"Oh, no, that's impossible," Anna protested. "Mrs. Hipper might not like that! But the children's breakfast nook would be the very place for her. Funny I didn't think of it right away. Come on, Madame, take off your things and I'll show you where it is."

Through the kitchen and the pantry and the dining room we went until we reached a large square hall with a wide marble stair-case and many doors.

"This way," said Anna, ushering me into a tiny dark room without any windows, where stood a table and four chairs. "Do sit down," she continued, switching on a lamp in the ceiling that made the little room look

[149]

ghastly in comparison with the golden light of the evening sun that flooded the hall outside. Mr. Brown, the chauffeur, had followed us, also Mr. Goodman.

"Sit down, boys," invited Anna affably, as she took a chair next to mine, "and Madame will tell us all about her trip, won't you, Madame?"

"Why, yes," I heard myself answer as in a dream, for everything that was happening to me then seemed so strange, so unreal, "just like Alice in Wonderland," I thought and wanted to say: "Curiouser and curiouser" aloud.

"Did you have a cabin all to yourself?" asked Mr. Goodman conversationally, lighting his cigarette and passing on the match to Mr. Brown. But before I could reply Kathleen came in with a tray, while Minnie closely followed her, calling out jovially:

"Look, Madame, see what a dainty supper I fixed for you in a jiffy! You must eat every bit of it."

"Oh, thank you, thank you," I cried desperately, feeling that I couldn't swallow a morsel and yet not wanting to hurt the kind soul's feelings. But at that moment Mr. Goodman, evidently unable to resist the habit of performing his duty whenever any food was being served, got up and putting aside his lighted cigarette elegantly took charge of the proceedings. By that time all the others had come in and as there were not enough chairs for every one to sit down, they remained standing by the wall, gravely looking at me as I frantically tried to eat. At last unable to go on I looked at Minnie in despair.

"Oh, your supper is so good, delicious," I cried, nearly choking, "but I am afraid that I am still train sick and cannot eat any more. Do you mind?"

"Oh, poor Madame, poor little Madame!" exclaimed Minnie pityingly, coming up and putting her plump arm around me. "Of course you are still giddy from such a long journey, of course. You'd better go up to your room and lie down."

"Up to her room?" inquired Anna shrilly, "up to her room, why, Minnie, what are you talking about? You know she hasn't any room here. She's to spend the night at the Dawn hotel and to-morrow Mrs. Hipper will take her to the boarding house."

A profound silence followed her words, then some one whispered audibly:

"It's a darn shame with all them empty guest rooms upstairs."

"Sh, sh," hissed Anna reprovingly, "now don't put any ideas into her head so soon. You know that Mrs. Hipper said that Mr. Brown was to drive her down to the hotel after she had had some supper. So if you've really finished, Madame, and don't feel like visiting with us any longer, I think you'd better go now."

"The hotel will suit me perfectly," I replied. "I

really don't feel very well and would like to go to bed, if I may."

"It's all right with me," declared Mr. Brown gallantly. "I'll drive you down there any time you wish. Come on, Madame, say good-night and we'll go right now, if that's what you want."

"Good-night," they all cried in chorus, while I got up and, murmuring a general good-night, followed Mr. Brown to the car—an enormous limousine that made me think of Noah's Ark.

"Pretty big, isn't she?" remarked Mr. Brown with pride as we drove away. "Seats eight passengers easily. Mr. Hipper had the body built especially for him at the factory and I must say they did a swell job. Cost him a lot of money too."

Down the shady avenue we went until we came again to the principal thoroughfare crowded with automobiles and street cars, where after driving for a while Mr. Brown turned to the left down a quiet street at the end of which stood the hotel.

"If you don't mind walking a few steps I'll park here," he said, stopping the car and helping me to alight.

"Park, what do you mean, park?" I asked, puzzled, not understanding what he was talking about. My ignorance seemed to amuse him very much, for he stared at me incredulously, then burst out laughing and, slapping his thigh, shouted:

"That's a real funny one, Madame! Why, don't they park their cars over there?"

"But a park is a place with trees and bushes," I tried to explain without any success, for he laughed harder than ever.

"Let me see, how shall I make it clear to you," he said, suddenly stopping and looking at me very seriously. "Oh, yes, in French it's parkay le automobile. Now do you understand?"

I didn't, but nodded wisely, which evidently satisfied him and without further explanations we came to the hotel. There Mr. Brown took me up to the desk and with a detached air of a man about town, introduced me to the clerk, saying:

"Mr. Boner, I want you to shake hands with Madame, our new French teacher; came all the way from the old country to-day. Madame, shake hands with Mr. Boner. Is her room ready? You know the one Mrs. Hipper engaged."

"Yeah, it's ready, all right," replied the clerk, coming out from behind his desk, and then, looking at me attentively, he put out his hand and declared: "Pleased to meet you, I'm sure." Then he asked me to register, and as I complied both he and Mr. Brown peered anxiously over my shoulder to see what I was writing.

When I had finished they looked at each other and smiled.

"That's a queer name," remarked Mr. Boner meditatively, "you sure will have to teach me how to pronounce it—couldn't say it now to save my life. But I can see that it's French, all right."

I hadn't the energy to contradict him and apparently quite satisfied with his knowledge of foreign names he led the way to the elevator, Mr. Brown, myself and a boy with my suitcases following, and then down a long dingy corridor to the room that he had said was ready for me. As he threw open the door with the traditional grand gesture of all clerks the world over, I could see that it was a very small room, though luckily a corner one with two windows, one of which overlooked a good-sized cascade formed by the river. That pleased me.

"It's real cool in here," he said, while Mr. Brown, tiptoeing in, cap in hand, murmured: "Say, this isn't bad at all. If you keep both windows open you'll even have some air."

"Yeah, it isn't bad if she doesn't mind the noise of the water," agreed Mr. Boner, putting up the window sashes, turning on the lights and opening closets with the wily air of a magician displaying his bag of tricks. "But, say," he continued, addressing Mr. Brown in a confidential undertone, "why didn't you put her up in the house? Didn't know as you had any guests over there now."

"We haven't any," replied Mr. Brown, looking somewhat embarrassed. He then coughed discreetly and winking broadly in my direction, said tactfully, "I'll tell you about that as we go down. Gotta be leavin' now anyhow. Good night, Madame, hope you'll be comfortable, pleasant dreams." And the next minute they were gone.

As I couldn't think of sleeping I turned the lights out and sat down by the window overlooking the cascade. Foaming and glittering in the transparent golden light of a midsummer evening it soon proved hypnotically soothing with its perpetual motion and everlasting roar, and as I sat staring at it, as usual, my thoughts turned to the past. I thought of home and of my childhood when teachers arrived in Troitskoe and my parents welcomed them on the doorstep. The guest rooms so carefully prepared for them were invariably filled with flowers that my mother always picked herself, making lovely nosegays which harmonized with the color scheme of the room. Many times before they arrived she would go upstairs to see if everything was prepared the way she wished it. The curly maple bedsteads, with their soft linen sheets smelling so fragrantly of lavender, the writing desks with their note paper stamped "Troitskoe," the washing stands bearing their

[155]

sets of basins and jugs of various sizes all marked with the Skariatine monogram, the chintz-covered furniture, the curtains and rugs and old etchings—all were placed by my mother with an eye for comfort and beauty.

"Now," she would say, putting her head on one side and looking around critically, "now I think it's all right." And then flicking away a speck of imaginary dust, or straightening the folds of a chintz curtain, or rearranging some flowers in a vase—would finally declare that everything was ready and that she'd go down to await their arrival.

"Run and call papa," she would say anxiously, "they will soon be here and he must not forget to greet them at the door."

Usually guests arrived in the late afternoon—about six o'clock, as the train that came to our station at four was the most convenient of all to travel by and then it took two hours for the horse-drawn carriages to cover the twenty miles from the station to the house. We could always hear the bells on the collars of the horses and the sound of their hoofs as they entered the great willow tree avenue or "Big Prospect" as it was called, and then we would all rush onto the colonnade in front of the main entrance and listen to the metallic clip-clop of the horse-shoes as they struck the road, so firm and hard during summer that it shone as though it were made of polished steel. Dinga linga, dinga linga, rang out the bells of the four horses, and that sound so typically Russian always made my heart stand still. And with each arrival the same scene was reënacted again: I can see it now so clearly.

"They're coming, they're coming," a scout posted on the road yells, as he runs towards us waving his arms, and then my father and mother gravely take up their places in the very center of the colonnade. Louder and louder comes the sound of hoofs and bells and the next minute the landau or victoria, or whatever other vehicle had been sent to the station, appears in a cloud of dust and smartly dashes up to the front door.

"Tpprrr," the coachman says to his horses, while Jacob, the butler, rushes forward to help the guest alight. Then my father and mother advance with outstretched hands, smiling and saying all the kind welcoming words they can think of. Then one by one we all approach and shake hands while the servants in the background bow low.

"Oh, you must be so tired," my mother says pityingly; "come to your room and rest before dinner. You have a whole hour, you know. And your bath is ready, and I'll send you a cup of hot tea."

Suddenly those visions of the past that I had been seeing in the white foam of the cascade vanished, and I realized that I was all alone and penniless in a hotel room of an unknown Middle Western town of America.

"Oh, oh," I groaned in a sudden paroxysm of despair, throwing myself on the bed and hiding my face in the pillow. "I can't stand it, I can't stand it," I cried in such a frenzy of anguish that even tears wouldn't come to my relief, and then, jumping up, rushed to the window overlooking the cascade.

"Now if only I had the courage to do it now, right now," I thought, staring at the swirling water below me. Then desperately, as though unconsciously taking leave of life I looked around the room for the last time, and as I did so, I suddenly caught sight of something I had not noticed before: a little black book lying on top of the chest of drawers.

"What can it be?" I wondered. And that new thought cutting like lightning through the haze of despair that had enveloped me created the psychological diversion that most decidedly saved my life. Turning away from the window and stumbling across the room, the eternal curiosity of Eve overcoming the suicidal urge, I reached out for the book. "Gideon's Bible," it said—nothing more, but the change in the trend of my thoughts had been accomplished and as I stood there holding the little black book and forgetting both window and cascade, I wondered who Gideon was—a publisher perhaps or a new interpreter of the Bible. Suddenly I felt terribly tired, and replacing the book on top of the chest of drawers, crept back to the bed where, stretching myself full length, I lay perfectly still in a state of half consciousness, half sleep that lasted all night long—unable to move or even raise a finger with the never-ceasing roar of the water in my ears—"as though I am drowning," I dully thought. When finally morning came I got up aching all over—as if I had been beaten and bruised. It took me a long time to bathe and dress, and only after I had had several cups of black coffee, did I feel somewhat better. Listlessly dragging myself back to the same window above the cascade I sat down on the edge of the bed and waited. At last as a clock in the distance struck nine, my telephone rang.

"Is this Madame?" came the familiar stuffy voice of the female Hipper right into my ear. "It is? Well, then, will you please come down at once,—I am in the lounge and cannot wait for you more than five minutes. And I've sent a boy up for your bags, so hurry!"

Frantically putting on my hat and grabbing my things I rushed downstairs. There in the lounge stood Mrs. Hipper looking as dissatisfied as ever while she peered at her diamond wrist watch.

"Bongjur," she said, as I came up gasping:

"Oh, how do you do, Mrs. Hipper?"

"Bongjur," she said again, then reprovingly: "Will you kindly speak only French, Madame! Remember it's nine o'clock and your duties have begun."

With the feeling that I had just been ducked in ice cold water I obediently replied:

"*Bon jour, Madame, comment allez vous?*" But she glared at me as though I were talking Chinese and then ordered me to speak slowly and distinctly and also to translate into English every word I said.

By this time we were going towards the huge car where sat Mr. Brown at the wheel looking straight ahead of him with the impassive face of the well-bred chauffeur. However, as I stood on the sidewalk waiting for Mrs. Hipper to get in, he suddenly winked one eye at me, as much as to say: "It's all right, I know who you are and would like to say hello, but you see it can't be done!"

Once seated in the car Mrs. Hipper turned towards me looking very displeased.

"Will you please talk and *keep* talking, Madame?" she said severely. "Remember I need to practice my French as much as possible and the more you talk the better."

Wildly I cudgeled my brains for some appropriate, clever and entertaining subject of conversation but couldn't think of a thing to say except a few inane words about the size of the car.

"Now translate the thought you've just expressed," said my employer with a look of dawning interest on her face—"eager to hear her French teacher's words of

[160]

MYSELF AT THE AGE OF FOUR

wisdom, poor thing," I thought as I lamely translated my idiotic remark, fully expecting to be reprimanded for it. But she nodded her head in a pleased way and said complacently: "Oah, wee, it's a very fine car, the best in town in fact, and cost Mr. Hipper a great deal of money," adding, "now say that in French," which I did, feeling more foolish than ever.

Our first stop was at a grocery store mysteriously called "Piggly-Wiggly" where Mrs. Hipper got out, motioning me to follow her, while Mr. Brown came behind me carrying a large basket. After entering the place we passed through a little wooden swing gate (amazingly there were no clerks in sight) and round the store we went in procession, Mrs. Hipper helping herself to all kinds of things which she told me to name in French as she put them into Mr. Brown's basket. When finally this tour of choosing and picking whatever Mrs. Hipper wanted was ended we came to another little wooden gate through which we were evidently supposed to exit, and here a woman in a blue smock looked over the purchases and presented a bill which Mrs. Hipper paid. After that we went back to the car and then drove to the overwhelming Hipper mansion. We stopped at the front entrance this time and I followed Mrs. Hipper into the house. Two little girls were playing in the hall, chasing each other around a long table that stood in the center of the room, while

Anna, their nurse, sat by watching them. As we came in they stopped running and stared at me with round eyes and open mouths.

"Shake hands with Madame, the French teacher," said Mrs. Hipper to them in an encouraging voice, but they didn't obey her and stood staring at me like two little owls. Then Anna came up to them and gave each a shake which proved more effective than Mrs. Hipper's request. The first to recover was Jennie, the elder, a child of about seven years with thin yellow hair, a pale narrow pointed face and strange-looking eyes that made me think immediately of a fox.

"Bongjur, Madame," she said, coming up to me, and smiling in a forced unnatural way put out a limp anemic little hand. Then that duty accomplished she turned towards her adopted mother and twisting her face into a persuasive grimace said ingratiatingly, "Oh, mother dear, I'm so glad to see you, and what have you brought me to-day?" While Mrs. Hipper crying delightedly, "Isn't she an angel?" clasped her to her much-bejeweled bosom. Then the other little girl came up led by Anna, and still staring at me with wide open eyes murmured something vague that must have been "bongjur." The second child, Bella, appealed to me at once. About four or five years old, chubby, rosy, with enormous violet blue eyes, golden hair and a real baby look about her, she reminded me of one of Raphael's cherubs, the one with the pensive eyes who gazes with such interest at the sinful earth below, as he (or she) leans out of heaven.

"You nice fat baby, you're the angel here," I wanted to say, and give her a hug, but remembering my position deemed it wiser not to show any feelings whatsoever. Then Anna greeted me primly, saying also "bongjur, Madame," in a precise and expressionless tone of voice as though she had never played the rôle of affable hostess towards me. Dreamily I stood in the middle of the hall, wondering what was going to happen next and at the same time taking in all the details of the amazing interior decorations. Strange pictures in heavy gilt frames, complicated pseudo antique pieces of furniture, silver ships with sails blowing out in an imaginary wind, a canary in a bright cage—all contributed to create the impression of a show room in a very expensive interior decorator's shop. And as Mrs. Hipper proudly led me from room to room that impression became stronger and stronger until I fully expected a suave salesman to appear and point out with a manicured finger every item of interest. But the climax of it all was the picture gallery with its collection of masterpieces. I went around in wonderment, while Mrs. Hipper impressively named each object and also the exorbitant price that had been paid for it. I could hardly believe that I wasn't "seeing and hearing things." At last we came to a bright little picture in a gaudy gilt frame.

"Now this is a Rembrandt," remarked Mrs. Hipper complacently, while I stared at her in amazement. "Mr. Hipper paid quite a little fortune for it," she continued, "but I don't think I should tell you how much it cost; he might not like that. Now translate all this into French."

Dutifully I complied and then we proceeded on our tour of inspection. Through the dining room and to the library which was the best room of all, with its white bookcases, large fire-place and leather arm chairs.

"Here is where we shall sit most of the time and study," announced Mrs. Hipper, and silently, but from the depths of my heart I thanked the Powers for that.

There were plenty of bedrooms upstairs, and while she took me through them I wondered again why I was not considered eligible to live in one of them. But that was a mystery that I was never to solve. When finally I had been shown all over the place Mrs. Hipper declared that it was time to study seriously and we returned to the library where she sat down in front of me and gravely said:

"Begin!"

"Begin what?" I felt like asking, while the foolish words:

"Begin at the beginning and stop at the end," flashed

through my mind. But I managed to look wise and answered gravely:

"Very well, let us begin."

Then for the next hour I pointed out all the various things that surrounded us, naming them in French and making her repeat every word after me, which she did very painstakingly. However towards the end of that lesson I could see that she was getting tired and sleepy and before the hour was over she had closed her eyes, opened her mouth and frankly fallen asleep in the way people do in trains. As long as I droned on: "an arm-chair—un fauteuil; a rug—un tapis," and so forth, she slept, but the minute I stopped she called out drowsily: "Go on, I hear you! Go on, I'm learning!" until I wondered if she memorized words in the way parrots do, during sleep.

Suddenly a frightful whistle shriekingly pierced the air, then another one joined it and another, until a veritable chorus of demoniacal whistles filled the room. Alarmed, I looked at Mrs. Hipper, fully expecting her to jump up in a panic, but she only stirred slightly, slowly opening her eyes with the fishy look of a sleeper just beginning to waken and merely remarked indistinctly as though her mouth were full of cereal:

"That's twelve o'clock. You'd better go and see about your lunch at the boarding house. Brown will take you in the car to-day and show you the way. Then this evening you can walk down there for dinner. Now ring the bell and tell Kathleen that I want him to bring the car around, and go and put your hat on."

With shaking fingers I obeyed, aghast at the thought of a new experience coming so soon on top of all the others. As I climbed into the car and was rapidly driven off to the mysterious place where I had to eat, Mr. Brown turned towards me encouragingly:

"Look here, Madame, don't you get blue. Your eyes are that round and scared that it makes a fellow feel bad himself. Honest, it does. I guess it's all pretty new and tough on you, but you'll get used to it all right. Can't see why the Missus won't let you eat at the house where there's plenty of food left over, but you mustn't mind that, the boarding house isn't such a bad place after all."

And with these consoling words he stopped the car in front of a two-storied, dingy yellow frame house that bore the inscription of "Bella Vista," in letters of tarnished gold against a black background, placed exactly above the front door.

"Here you are, Madame, it's all right, buck up," he whispered, as he helped me to get out. "And, oh, say," he cried, as I was about to enter the house, "I'll come and get you in an hour and won't ask any one either if I can," he added, significantly jerking his thumb in the probable direction of the Hipper residence. I nodded gratefully with what I trusted was a bright smile, but what most likely wasn't anything of the kind. Then with a sinking heart I entered the boarding house. In a small hall, at the foot of the golden oak staircase, sat a few people in cane rockers all rocking violently and looking anxiously in the direction of a closed door, through which came the unmistakable clatter of dishes being handled none too carefully. No one paid the slightest attention to my entrance and seeing that there wasn't anything for me to sit on, I went up to the wall and leaned against it. Silence reigned for a few minutes, then:

"Where are the eats?" suddenly shouted an old fellow in shirt sleeves. His gray trousers were held up by red suspenders, and a pair of golden spectacles perched dangerously on the very tip of his nose.

"Yes, where *are* the eats?" chimed in another voice, female this time, and looking around I saw that it belonged to a tall, thin, unusually homely woman of about thirty-five, with a face like a horse, heavily powdered and rouged, surmounted by a marcelled wig that was so frankly, so blatantly a wig, without the slightest attempt at trying to appear natural, that it was quite embarrassing.

"Why doesn't she make it look like real hair, poor thing?" I wondered, but to judge by the self-satisfied

[167]

smirk on her face she evidently was so pleased with herself that my pity was quite misplaced.

"Eats," I thought interestedly, "they both said 'eats,'—I haven't heard that word used in that way before," and then decided to try not to forget to put it in my little note book where I wrote down methodically all the expressions and old words with new meanings such as: "attaboy, guy, park," and others that I was now hearing every day, coining carefully and learning with great rapidity. At that point a group of young men in greasy overalls burst into the house singing lustily to the tune of "Over There":

> *"The guys are coming, the guys are coming*
> *With a rum tum tumming in their 'tums."*

Instantly all the other people joined in the song, and for the next few minutes the noise was terrific. Then the door that every one had been watching so anxiously was thrown open and an enormous woman in a loose, blue gingham dress and with skimpy hair tied in a knot on top of her head appeared on the threshold and in a loud voice announced:

"Come on, folks, food's on!"

Whereupon there was a general stampede for the dining room, each person making a definite rush for a certain chair. As I stood wondering where my place would be, the big woman suddenly noticed me.

"Hello, stranger," she cried, coming up to me and looking me over from head to foot. "Are you the French woman from the Hippers'? You are? Well, my name is Mrs. Pance and I am the lady who runs this place. Pleased to meet you, I'm sure. Now let me see, where shall I put you? Guess you might as well sit between Mr. Holl" (she pointed to the old gentleman with the red suspenders) "and Mr. Duty—they won't be too naughty if you don't let them, but they'll try, they'll try,—specially Mr. Holl. He's a hot one."

"What's that?" queried the old fellow, wheeling around on his chair and gazing at me over his spectacles. But she motioned him to be quiet.

"Now what's *your* name?" she asked. "I've got to introduce you to the folks. Speak up, girl."

"My name is Madame de Keller," I answered in a low voice, whereupon she turned towards her guests all busily munching and shouted in tones that were probably heard all down the street.

"Folks, I want ye to meet Mrs. DuKenny, the French marm who's gone to work for the Hippers. Come on now, everybody, give her a welcome!" And they all obediently cried:

"Hello, Mrs. DuKenny, pleased to meet you!"

Bewildered, not knowing what I was expected to answer, I gasped faintly: "How do you do," and dropped into the chair between Mr. Holl and Mr.

Duty. For a few seconds every one stared at me attentively, then food was attacked once more and I was forgotten. The first course consisted of a slice of tough cold meat, with potato salad, pickles and beets all heaped together on one plate. Feeling very hungry I decided to ignore the toughness of the meat and was trying my best to cut it when all of a sudden I heard a queer sound next to me, and, looking up, saw Mr. Holl violently red, with his fingers in his mouth, desperately choking.

"Oh," I cried in alarm, "he's choking, look!" But no one was paying the slightest attention to him and the next minute he was all right again, triumphantly holding his set of false teeth in one hand while with the other he reached for his glass of water.

"There," he exclaimed, carefully dropping the teeth into the glass, "that's better. Funny thing," he went on, turning towards me, "every time I forget to take them teeth out I start chokin' this way. Next time be a good girl and remind me, will you? Miss Biggs, who used to sit by me, on that very same chair that you're sittin' on, always hollered, 'teeth' before we began eatin', and then I'd recollect and take them out. You see my gums are stronger and chew better than them darn old teeth."

He seemed a kindly, harmless old man, but after

the episode with his teeth I didn't feel like eating any more and put down my knife and fork.

"What's the matter?" asked Mr. Duty, my other neighbor, "don't you like the meat? It's good to-day," he continued appreciatively, and relapsed into munching silence again. Then, when he had assuaged his hearty appetite he turned towards me once more. "Say, Missus, sorry I've forgotten your name, never could remember French names even when I was over there; I know what's the matter with you; you're homesick, blue! How about going with me to the movies to-night, what do you say?"

Again I was puzzled.

"Movies, what's that—movies?" I asked, feeling stupidly ignorant and hoping that no one else heard my question.

Mr. Duty glanced at me in surprise but didn't laugh. "Don't you know," he said in a low voice, evidently wishing to spare me any public humiliation. "Why, movies are a show, a picture show that moves like this on a screen." And he obligingly waved his hand, palm side towards me, in front of my face to demonstrate how the pictures moved.

"Oh, cinema, you mean the cinema," I cried delightedly, while Mr. Duty, evidently relieved at having explained the mysterious word so successfully, nodded his head with satisfaction.

"Cinema! That's right, that's what you call it over there; I forgot. But didn't I tell you that I always forget French names? And there you are, I've done it again. But how about it—will you go with me to-night?"

"No, thank you, Mr. Duty," I replied as politely as I could, for he too, like old Mr. Holl, seemed very kindly and earnest. "You see," I went on, "I have to work all day and I will be too tired to do anything in the evenings."

"Well, perhaps some Saturday afternoon," he suggested, and I murmured vaguely, "Perhaps."

Meanwhile every one around the table grew increasingly noisy. Conversation was carried on in loud shouts and the young men in overalls had begun to sing again, at the same time trying their hardest to pinch the seat of the plump young daughter of the Pance household, a very fair maiden with an upturned nose and flashing teeth who dodged and giggled and slapped her swains whenever they succeeded in nipping her as she waited on them.

"Why, Marygold-Rose, I'm surprised at you!" her mother exclaimed several times reprovingly, though obviously unable to conceal her maternal pride at her daughter's undeniable success.

Under cover of all that noise I turned to Mr. Duty and asked him to tell me about each person at the table. He seemed quite pleased at my request and exclaiming:

[172]

"Always glad to oblige a lady!" started to describe. "On your left is Mr. Holl," he began, while I nodded sagaciously, "he is an artist, a real artist one might say, a painter."

"Oh, really," I cried interestedly, "and what does he paint?"

"Walls," answered Mr. Duty gravely, "he does the best job in town, painting walls. Just lays on the paint like butter; never a streak, never a blotch anywhere— elegant I call it! Then next to him is Mr. Rover, a traveling salesman, smart as a whip. He has been all over this country and Mexico too. Then that young fellow with the red face is a gasoline tank driver, and the lady next to him is his wife." (Here he pointed surreptitiously at the female with the wig.) "Now the old couple across the table are Mr. and Mrs. Kabb; he was in the lumber business and is retired now. The young fellow facing you is a tobacco salesman and the little blond is his wife. They're just married and have been here only a week, honeymooning. And those boys," he continued, taking in with a sweep of his hand all the young men in overalls, "work in the railroad shops. Mighty fine fellows, all of them. Well, now I've told you about everybody, haven't I?"

"And how about yourself?" I asked, "you've forgotten that."

Mr. Duty blushed, and his shiny round face with its

round nose, round black eyes, wide mouth and black hair sticking up on end, suddenly appeared very young.

"There isn't much to tell about me," he said modestly, looking to see if any one was listening. He then went on in a confidential undertone, "I'm a potter by profession and also in the fireworks business. Oh, say!" he continued, forgetting his self-consciousness and becoming excited as a sudden thought struck him, "say, will you come and see when I shoot the fireworks at the County Fair? It's elegant, ma'am, elegant! No other Fair can beat our fireworks. I've heard people say that, and they've traveled all over the country, like Mr. Rover, fr'instance. You'll come, won't you? I'll get you a good seat right in front of everybody and you can watch me shoot the darn fool things off, rockets and pinwheels and all. It's a sight you mustn't miss, Madmozell. Bang go the rockets, and fizz go the wheels, and then we have a blazing sun and all kinds of pictures and the American flag at the finish. And I am the man who does it all, chief man, I mean. I've got lots of help, of course. Oh, it's grand!" And the little fellow sighed ecstatically.

The dessert, a rather tasty cherry pie, was cleared away. The gasoline tank driver's wife got up from the table, stretching herself luxuriously and yawning, while the old lumber lady hiccoughed loudly and then turning towards Mrs. Pance remarked in a satisfied voice:

"My, but I'm full!"

As I left the dining room I could hear one of the railroad boys call out in a thin falsetto voice:

"By, by, Frenchy, be a good girl and don't do anything I wouldn't do!" while the others broke into a roar of laughter. Running out I found Mr. Brown sitting on the porch reading a newspaper and waiting for me.

"Hello, Madame," he said, getting up and smiling in a friendly fashion. "Here I am, all set to take you back to the house. And it's just as well I came; you're a bit late you know."

"The dinner lasted so long," I said, anxiously wondering if Mrs. Hipper would scold me. When I got back she was waiting for me on the sofa with a wet towel around her head and a glass of ice-cold lemonade in her hand.

"You are twelve minutes late; translate that into French," she remarked as I entered the room, apologizing. "And translate into English what you're answering too. Then daypayshay-voo—I found that in my grammar book while I was waiting for you—and go on with your lesson."

On and on through the hot afternoon I droned, while she listened and dozed, my head aching desperately and my mouth and throat feeling parched and strange. The hands on the elaborate marble clock that stood in the center of the mantelpiece seemed as sluggish as everything else that sultry afternoon and several times I had to twist my fingers painfully to keep from falling asleep too. I'd stare at the clock in silent anguish and then say to myself: "I won't look at it again for half an hour." But when I thought that the half hour was over and would glance up hopefully, I'd see with despair that only five minutes had passed.

"If this goes on much longer I'll scream," I thought, and then wondered what would happen if I really did give vent to a piercing shriek. "What a relief that would be," I went on thinking pleasantly. Of a sudden I burst out laughing at the mental picture I saw of Mrs. Hipper's surprise if it actually happened.

"What's the matter?" asked the real Mrs. Hipper, waking up and looking at me severely as she raised herself into a sitting posture on the sofa, her fuzzy dyed hair all awry and her face slightly swollen on the side she had been lying on. "Why do you laugh, Madame? I don't see anything to laugh at!"

"Only a funny story that I suddenly remembered," I answered, trying to stop laughing and, to my dismay, not succeeding.

"Well, if it's so amusing, tell it to me; I like funny stories," she said, once more arranging herself comfortably on her pillows and looking at me like an expectant owl. "You can tell it in English first and then translate it into French," she added considerately.

Wildly I racked my brain for a funny story and could not think of one to save my life.

"It's only funny in French and can't be translated; it would lose its point," I stammered. But she wouldn't be put off. She wanted a funny story and by the determined look on her face, a look that was becoming quite familiar to me, I saw that she meant to have it too.

"Well, it's like this," I began, not knowing what I was going to say next, and still trying frantically to think of something funny. "And after all it isn't a French story at all, but a Greek one, ancient and historic," I continued, suddenly remembering with joy a nonsensical thing that my sister used to tell me when I was small. This is it: "One day Themistocles went for a stroll and suddenly came face to face with an enemy of his. 'Aha!' exclaimed the prudent Themistocles loudly, 'aha! You want to kill me, do you?' And with these wise words he rapidly disappeared around the corner."

"Is that all?" asked Mrs. Hipper, still staring at me expectantly as though she was sure that there was more to follow.

"That's all," I answered, feeling somewhat abashed, as I realized that my story wasn't anything to laugh oneself sick over.

"Well, then, I don't think much of it," declared Mrs. Hipper disapprovingly, "and what's more I cannot say that you have a strong sense of humor, either."

"Oh, but, Mrs. Hipper," I protested, "it really is awfully funny in Greek, but I told you that it would lose all its good points when translated."

"Well, you were right," she said, "and I'm disappointed in you. I thought you'd tell me a lot of funny French stories. That was one of the reasons that I hired you. But if they're all as funny as the one you've just told me, you may keep them to yourself. And now before dinner Brown will take you to the place where you're going to sleep."

"Another place!" I gasped in dismay, my heart sinking into my shoes once more. "Oh, where am I going now?"

"You're going to see the room I've engaged for you in Mrs. Daisy Whopple's house. It's a very nice room and will cost you only thirty dollars a month."

"Cost *me?*" I cried, "do I have to pay for my room and board out of my salary?"

"Indeed you do!" answered Mrs. Hipper decidedly. "We pay you a hundred and twenty-five dollars a month and you should be able to save quite a lot of money out of that: thirty for your room and thirty for your meals—that leaves you sixty-five dollars clear, a very nice sum for you, I should say. If I am satisfied with you I may help you out with the meals, but I haven't made up my mind about that yet—it depends entirely on your work. Now go along with Brown to Mrs. Whopple's house, and then from there you can walk to Bella Vista for your dinner. After that you will come back here. If we are still at table you can wait in the library."

"You horrible, nasty, cruel, cold-blooded, wicked old woman!" I thought furiously, as I got into the car. "You've been beastly to me all day! You never even greeted me properly, or asked me whether I had a nice journey, or whether I was tired!—Nothing, not a kind word. And now I have to sleep in one place because you don't think I'm fit to live in your house, and eat in another, and pay for it all out of the wretched little sum you give me! And on top of everything you have had the cruelty to show me all your pictures and tell me: 'This one cost fifteen thousand dollars and that one twenty-five thousand.' Oh, how I hate you, hate you, hate you!"

Though that mental outburst relieved my pent-up feelings, still I was trembling all over when we reached Mrs. Whopple's house. Mr. Brown, after one anxious glance at my face, seemed to realize that words were of no avail and opened the door in silence. However as I was getting out, he said gently:

"I'll wait for you, Madame, and take you down to Mrs. Pance's. And don't hurry, I've plenty of time."

Feeling socialistic and bolshevistic and anarchistic to the very marrow of my bones I walked slowly towards the house thinking: "Only the poor, working people have been kind to me. As for that Hipper millionairess —how I would love to see her in the midst of a good old Revolution, that would burn her pictures and destroy her house and confiscate her jewels and money and make her work! Yes, that's what she needs—work to make her human."

On the porch I barely avoided a collision with a tall heavy boy of about fifteen who did not step aside to let me pass, though he was standing right in my way in front of the door, staring at me with a queer vacant look in his eyes.

"Is Mrs. Whopple at home?" I asked, thinking how strange he seemed, but he didn't answer and only stared at me the harder.

"Is she at home?" I repeated louder, wondering if perhaps he was deaf, but again he only stared. Then he broke into a loud chuckle and pointing his finger at me said rapidly:

"Who, who, who, who? . . ." in a loud guttural voice, at the same time waving his arms up and down and hopping on one leg in a state of great excitement.

"Oh, poor boy," I thought, and making myself

as small as possible so as not to push him aside, slid past him into the house. At first I could not distinguish anything as the place after the bright light out of doors seemed to be plunged in utter darkness, but gradually my eyes became accustomed to the change and I saw that I was standing in a very small hall at the foot of another golden oak staircase, similar to the one in Mrs. Pance's house. Not knowing what to do next, I called out, "Is Mrs. Whopple at home?" in a rather quavering voice that didn't sound like mine. To my relief some one immediately shouted back, "Here I am," very briskly, and then the owner of the voice appeared in the doorway, again a large woman dressed also in a blue gingham dress.

"Golden oak staircases, big women, blue gingham dresses—everything seems to repeat itself here," I thought as she came up to me smiling and saying:

"Good evening. Mrs. Hipper just phoned me that you were on your way. Your room is all ready for you, come right up."

And up a narrow stairway we went, until we came to a tiny landing that led into a short dark corridor with doors on both sides.

"Here is your room," said my landlady, opening the first door to the left and leading the way in.

It was small and square, with a faded gray wall-paper, a very large metal bedstead that occupied more than two-thirds of its space, a dresser, a chest of drawers, a table and chair—all of which had once been painted white. At the foot of the bed was the one and only window, which looked straight into another window that belonged to the house next door and through which I could see a large victrola.

"If I slide halfway down the bed, I'll be able to put my feet through my window and then if I slide further down and reach the sill, I'll perhaps be able to put my feet into the window of the other house," I thought, while Mrs. Whopple was carefully explaining to me how comfortable I would be.

"The bathroom is right down the corridor to the left," she said, "and as my children and I have our own bathroom, you'll share yours only with Mr. Pond, our other boarder. He's a very nice young man and I'm sure you two will get on grandly together. Now is there anything else that you would like to know?"

"No, thank you," I replied, "but if you don't mind I think I'll take a bath and change my dress for dinner."

"Oh, but there isn't any hot water yet, it's too early!" she exclaimed, looking at me in surprise, and seeming much relieved when I explained that I would take a cold bath.

"Oh, that's all right, that's all right, suit yourself," she cried, smiling hospitably again and obligingly leaving the room.

Discouraged I sank down on the edge of the bed and looked around me. On the wall a side light was dismally hanging out of its socket, an unpleasant, sickening odor of gas pervaded the room and the victrola, that stood in the window of the house next door, suddenly blared forth the doleful strains of "Yes, we have no bananas" so loudly that one might have thought that it was playing in my room.

"Not only bananas but we haven't anything to-day; plain old nothin'," I thought as I closed the window, lowered the shade and started to undress. And all the time while I bathed and got into fresh clothes the victrola kept up its maddening banana song, until I felt like reaching out of my window, grabbing it and smashing it to pieces. As soon as I was ready I ran downstairs and once more Mr. Brown kindly drove me to Bella Vista. Dinner was in full swing when I arrived and Mrs. Pance greeted me with loud cries of:

"Now, now Mrs. DuKenny, you're late, and don't you do that again! Marygold-Rose can't keep waiting on all of you separately. Dinner's at six, and at six you've gotta be here. Understand?"

"Yes, Mrs. Pance," I said meekly, sliding into my chair between Mr. Holl and Mr. Duty, while Marygold-Rose with a look of disdain brought me in a plate of soup.

"Don't do that again," whispered Mr. Duty anxiously, "it always makes her mad when any one's late,—awful mad," he added, solemnly shaking his head. Then Mr. Holl turned to me.

"Where you been, Madmozell?" he asked reproachfully. "I nearly swallowed me teeth again, all because you weren't here to remind me." But then seeing how sorry I was, he relented and told me a long story about himself when he was young. Dinner over, I walked back to the Hippers' and found them both sitting in the library drinking coffee.

"Hello, Madame," said Mr. Hipper, rising as I came in and shaking hands with me. "And how are you? Haven't seen you since you arrived. Did you have a good trip? I was going to Metropole to meet you yesterday but just missed the train. Hope you had a comfortable night."

"She's all right, Hiram," interrupted Mrs. Hipper before I could say a word. She had been watching us anxiously and seemed much annoyed at Mr. Hipper's cordial attitude.

"I think, Madame," she continued, a red spot appearing on each cheek, and her face twitching nervously, "that I won't need you any more this evening. You may go now and be sure to be here on time to-morrow morning at eight o'clock sharp. Good night."

"Good night," I answered, preparing to go, but Mr.

Hipper, with an obstinate look on his face, put out a detaining hand.

"One minute," he said peremptorily, "I want you to give me French lessons too. Nine o'clock every morning for half an hour will suit me fine; how about you?"

"Why, yes, that will suit me too, unless Mrs. Hipper has other plans for me," I replied, looking at her inquiringly. She flushed a deeper red mumbling:

"That's all right, have your lesson at nine," and waved her hand at me as much as to say, "Go now, go!"

"I don't see, Bella, why you didn't give her a room in this house," I heard him say as I was passing through the hall on my way out, but her answer never reached my ears. Slowly I walked down the street to Mrs. Whopple's house with the wretched feeling of having lived in this town all my life.

"And only the first day is ended," I thought. "How can I stand it for a whole year? Three hundred and fifty days like this one and what will I be like?"

As I approached the house that was to be my home for that appalling year, I heard the neighbor's victrola going full blast and coming closer realized with horror that it was still playing the same banana song. Desperately I gazed up at the window from where the unwelcome sounds were pouring forth with such volume and then decided that it was no use going up to my

room where I knew that the noise would only be ampli-
fied, as in an out-door orchestra shell.

"I'll go for a walk instead," I thought, and went on
down the street.

"You, you, you!" cried the unfortunate boy, waving
his arms at me from the porch as I passed the house,
"You, you. . . ." Evidently he was upset because I was
not coming in and, perhaps thinking that I had forgotten where I lived, was trying as best he could to tell
me that this was the house.

"It's all right; I'll soon be back; I'm only going
for a walk," I called out to him, and instantly he
quieted down, though he continued to crane his neck
and follow me with anxious eyes. I still did not know
who he was but supposed that he must be Mrs. Whopple's son. Evidently he lived in this house, and she had
spoken to me of her children.

"I do hope they're not all as peculiar," I sighed, and
continued to walk on.

The wide street called Jackson Avenue was quite
attractive with its tall shady trees and pleasant-looking
homes set far back from the sidewalk. Nice little lawns
lay between the walk and the houses while back of them
I could distinguish gardens with many flowers. The hot
air was beginning to cool off; a breeze had arisen and
the leaves rustled gently overhead. On and on I went
past many houses with their lamps all lighted and their

window shades up, so that I could see clearly everything inside. It was amusing to look in as I passed slowly along and to note the more or less uniform arrangements of all the living rooms. A fire-place, a big arm chair with a table and lamp next to it, and a man reading a newspaper, a cottage piano, a victrola, a radio, a davenport, a large table with a lamp in its middle and another arm chair with a woman reading or sewing. Nearly everywhere there was music—either the woman was playing the piano and singing jazz, or else the victrola or the radio was going full blast. Four times I heard the banana song and fled. But I didn't see any children anywhere and decided they were all in bed, for at times the squeal of a baby would come through the darkened window of an upper story and then the woman would get out of her arm chair and run towards the door. And as I went on and on I gradually began to feel like a ghost passing mysteriously down the street and gazing through windows at Life inside the houses. At last I came to the end of the avenue, to a field that in the dark appeared boundless as it stretched out towards the horizon and joined the starlit dome of the sky. Myriads of fireflies danced over the field and the night air was fragrant with unseen flowers. Tired out I was about to sink onto the grass when suddenly I noticed a large log next to where I stood.

"This is my home, my house," I thought as I sat down on it, "the only house I possess in the whole world," and then because I had had such a hard day and was weary and heavy at heart, I began to cry, and cried for a long while. Then, when I couldn't cry any more, I sat staring into the endless spaces above and below me, alive with the light of stars and fireflies. It seemed to me that I had reached the end of the world and had stopped on its very brink to gaze into the unknown Beyond, with its spheres of light, some large as Jupiter, some small as the tiniest firefly's speck of flame.

"If I leap now, I'll leave the earth and disappear into the ether, into eternity," I thought, and that thought made me feel giddy as though I were actually standing on the edge of the world. Time passed, the waning moon rose, and stiff and aching in every limb I got up from my log.

"Good-by, my House of Tears," I said aloud as I turned to go. "Good-by for to-night. But I'll come back here every evening as long as I stay in this town."

On the way back I walked quickly, for it was late and the lights in nearly all the windows were out and the street was dark and lonely. Coming to a cross street not far from Mrs. Whopple's house I suddenly heard the loud clanging of a bell, followed by a gleaming shaft of light that nearly blinded me. Instinctively I stopped and the next minute an enormous engine of a train loomed up right in front of me on the sidewalk and then slowly proceeded to cut across the street, creaking and rattling and groaning as it went followed by a long line of dark freight cars. Never before having seen a train cross a street I thought I was the victim of an hallucination, and cold with terror broke into a run, never once stopping or looking back until I had reached the house where my room was. With shaking fingers I thrust my key into the lock, opened the door and dashing up the stairs threw myself onto the bed, trembling from head to foot. I thought I could still hear the sinister clanging of that ghost-like bell in the distance and terror-stricken lay for a long while with the bed clothes pulled over my head and my fingers in my ears, wondering if that apparition had been a summons and if my death, like Anna Karenina's, was near at hand. Only at daybreak as the pale light of dawn began to filter into my room I fell asleep utterly broken in body and soul.

VII

THE next morning at seven, when my alarm clock rang I could hardly move, and again, as on the previous day at the Dawn hotel, I washed and dressed with painful difficulty. At a quarter to eight I started out to the Hippers' residence and five minutes later entered their house. In the hall I met Anna and the two little girls, looking fresh and clean after an apparently good night's rest. Then I caught a glimpse of myself in the mirror and saw with a start that I looked more like a scarecrow than anything else.

"Good morning, Madame," said Anna cheerfully, "you're to have your breakfast always with us, you know. Mrs. Hipper said last night that she forgot to speak to you about it and asked me to tell you. Also she said that she wishes you to speak French to us at breakfast so that the children and I can learn it too."

"All right," I agreed drearily, and followed her into the same little windowless dining room where I had had my first supper. To begin with the children were shy and wouldn't answer me, but soon the new words amused them and they repeated them after me, chirruping and chattering like two little magpies. Anna took her first lesson very seriously and, watching my lips attentively, tried hard to pronounce the words correctly.

After breakfast Mrs. Hipper called me into the library and there I remained until nine o'clock when Anna came in to say that Mr. Hipper was waiting for me. I was feeling very ruffled and upset again, for Mrs. Hipper had just been scolding me for all the newspaper publicity that I had received the previous day.

"Didn't I tell you, Madame, that I did not want any one to know that you had a title," she grumbled, "and then you go and tell all about it to the reporters and they plaster your name over the front pages of all the newspapers!"

And though I tried to explain to her how it happened, and how they had found out who I was from the Purser, she wouldn't listen to me and only became angrier and more unpleasant every minute.

"One of those reporters even had the nerve to come here," she said indignantly, "and of all things, he wanted your picture! But I sent him flying and, believe me, he won't come back in a hurry."

So after that talk I was in no frame of mind to be amiable to any one and answered Mr. Hipper's cordial "Hello, Madame, and how are you this fine day?" with a curt "Good morning" and a nod. Painstakingly we both went through the first chapter of the Berlitz School book but were interrupted several times by the mysterious appearance of Mrs. Hipper who tripped up so noiselessly in her sneakers and then peered around the door with such suspicion that finally her husband lost his temper and shouted angrily:

"What's the matter with you, and what do you want?" Jumping up, he closed the book with a bang, and dashed after her into the hall. There I could hear his voice saying something loudly and furiously though what exactly it was I did not grasp nor did I care to. But I was glad to hear that she was being scolded and wished with all my heart that he would spank her too.

Presently the front door closed with a bang, and Anna who had evidently been eavesdropping, came onto the porch where I was still sitting and whispered significantly:

"He's gone now, but my what a talking to he gave her! She's crying. Don't go in there 'til she calls you and don't mind her if she's mad. She's often that way; jealous, you know."

"Jealous of whom? Of me?" I cried in amazement, and nearly burst out laughing, but she waved her hands at me and exclaiming, "Ss-sh, be quiet or you'll get yourself in trouble and me, too," tiptoed off the porch. There I must have sat for about an hour or more, until Mr. Goodman appeared and with a formal bow but with an informal whisper:

"Come on, Madame, the show's over, she's all right now," told me that I was to go to her in the library at once. I found Mrs. Hipper reclining on her couch with swollen eyes and a tear-stained face.

"Serves you right," I thought vindictively, but then seeing how bedraggled and old and forlorn she looked, I suddenly felt sorry for her and decided to cheer her up.

"I've got an idea," I cried as brightly as I could. "Instead of telling you just words that bore you to death and tire you, I'll read to you aloud from some amusing French book. First just one sentence that I'll translate while you write down the new words; then I'll read it in French once again. How would you like that?"

She seemed very pleased with my invention, and finding an old book of Dumas, asked me to begin at once. Soon I noticed that my system was working successfully, that she memorized the words astonishingly well for a woman of her age and seemed much interested in the book. So then I decided to continue that way all the time, which I did until the very end. The results were most gratifying, for when my year in Dawn was over she could read and write and talk in French quite fluently. The little girls and Anna learned it too, but I never had another lesson with Mr. Hipper.

And so my days settled down to a humdrum routine. Up at seven with the alarm clock ringing violently, breakfast with Anna and the children and then the undiluted companionship of Mrs. Hipper until bed time, with only two intervals when I had lunch and dinner at the boarding house. Sometimes, though very rarely, she would let me go home before dinner and then I was free all evening, but mostly she made me return to her after dinner and kept me till it was time to go to bed. In that way I was with her from eight o'clock in the morning until ten or eleven and sometimes even twelve o'clock at night, reading, always reading Dumas's books aloud as she didn't care for any others. Never have I known such mental boredom! Then came a time when my eyes got weak and I needed glasses and my voice became husky and my throat was painful and sore. Then one day while I was reading a blood vessel broke and I had a throat hemorrhage and had to go to the hospital. But all that happened later on. Soon after I arrived I received letters from people

[195]

in Metropole who were acquainted with friends of mine in England and who having heard from them that I was in Dawn, invited me to their homes for the week ends. But Mrs. Hipper never let me go anywhere, and with one or two exceptions I stayed in Dawn without moving. Strangely enough, Mrs. Hipper had very few callers even though she had lived most of her life in Dawn, and I often wondered what was the reason. Was she ashamed of her old friends now that she was so rich and lived in such a grand house, and did she keep away from them deliberately (like Maggie in the cartoon of "Bringing up Father") or was she simply unpopular?

One day, however, about a month after my arrival a neighbor of Mrs. Hipper's, a Mrs. Milton, came to invite her to her daughter's wedding, and as I was of course in the room she politely invited me too.

"Thank you, I would very much like to come," I answered eagerly. "You know I've never been to an American wedding before and would be very interested to see one."

"Well, then, that's settled and we'll be delighted to have you," said Mrs. Milton pleasantly.

"And you must come to the reception at our house afterwards and to the dinner dance."

"Oh, Madame cannot go to that," interrupted Mrs. Hipper, looking very annoyed, "she may go to the church but that will be quite enough for her. There's absolutely no necessity of inviting her to your house, none whatsoever."

Mrs. Milton reddened and saying good-by rather abruptly rose to leave while I stood speechless with anger. As soon as Mrs. Milton left I turned to Mrs. Hipper.

"I am sorry that I cannot go on reading to-day," I said, controlling myself as best I could, though she probably saw how upset I was. "I have a bad headache and must lie down."

"All right," she answered frowning, "all right, you may go now and rest for a while, but be sure and be back in an hour; I'll be waiting for you." And she walked out of the room, slamming the door behind her to show that she was displeased with me for having a headache. But on the day of the wedding she suddenly became more amiable and even told me that I could drive down to the church with her in her car.

"And I have an old wrap I can lend you," she said quite graciously when she saw that I wasn't wearing any.

When we arrived at the church she whispered something to a tall young man who advanced to meet us.

"Oh, all right, Mrs. Hipper," he answered, glancing at me, and then beckoned to another young man wearing a flower like his own to come up. "Put her in a seat," he said in a low voice, but loud enough for me to hear him, and then, having disposed of me, proceeded to lead Mrs. Hipper up the aisle. The young man who had been told to place me somewhere, somehow, decided not to bother with me long and waving a white gloved hand loftily motioned me into a seat in the back row next to which I had been standing. Quietly I sat down, only too glad to have been given a place at last, and then looked around me. The church was prettily decorated with flowers and the light summer dresses of the women added a gay touch of color to the dark pews. The organ was playing softly, and a low buzz of voices filled the scented air. I could see Mr. and Mrs. Hipper sitting grandly in the front row and then, looking at the sea of unknown faces around me, I thought how strange it was to be in a town where I didn't know a single soul except the Hippers, the Whopples and the inmates of the boarding-house. But as my gaze wandered unconsciously over all those unfamiliar and not particularly interesting faces, I suddenly noticed with a start the face of a young woman that arrested my attention and appealed to me the very instant that I saw it. Small, lovely, with great luminous brown eyes full of intelligence, it stood out in that crowd like a beautiful flower surrounded by weeds. She was looking at me with a half smile that seemed to say shyly:

"And who are you? I've never seen you before. But I like you. Do you like me?"

And instinctively I smiled back. It was like seeing an

old friend in a crowd of strange people and for the first time since my arrival I felt that after all I was not alone in this dreary town. And so we kept looking at each other and smiling, just like two very small girls who want to become acquainted.

"Let us 'quaint!" my mother often told me that I used to say when I was little and wished particularly to know a child that attracted me. And "let us 'quaint" was what I felt like saying to that lovely young woman in the church. But suddenly there was a commotion outside, the congregation became silent, the organ began to play the Wedding March and the bridal procession entered the church. It was all very nice and pretty except the way they all walked up the aisle—"just like a slow motion goose-step," I thought, and I was so disagreeably affected by its unnaturalness and absurdity that I even looked away in another direction. Unaccountably things of that kind have always had the power of giving me little shivers down my spine and to this day I hasten to close my eyes when I see the ridiculous goose-step of a bridal procession. When the short ceremony was over, and I was wondering what was to become of me, Mrs. Hipper suddenly appeared and putting a fifty cent coin into my hand said:

"Take a taxi and go home now, and wait for me. I cannot take you back with me in the car because I'm going to the reception." Then she disappeared, leaving me standing in the pew tightly clasping the fifty cents. As I stepped into the aisle the pushing, jostling crowd carried me rapidly towards the entrance door and soon I found myself on the sidewalk and then in a taxi, panting a little, but glad to be out of the scramble. At the house I waited in vain for Mrs. Hipper's return and only saw her for a brief moment before dinner when she came in to change her dress for the wedding party.

"You are free this evening, Madame," she called out as she went upstairs, and terrified lest she should change her mind as well as her dress I ran out of the house as fast as my legs could carry me. That evening I went for a long walk and before ending up at the House of Tears as I did regularly every night, I decided to have a look at the Miltons' dance which I knew was being held in their garden. I could hear the music far down the street and as I cautiously approached their hedge I could see that the garden was gayly decorated with Japanese lanterns. A large wooden platform probably erected especially for that occasion served the purpose of a dance floor. It was a very pretty sight and as I stood gazing at it and humming the tune that the orchestra was playing, I suddenly recognized the lovely young woman whom I had seen at the wedding. She was dressed in white and silver and looked like a fairy— small, dainty and light-footed as she danced with a portly older man who seemed inordinantly proud of her. Just as they were passing very close to me I felt some one pinch me, and turning around saw the beaming face of Kathleen, the little parlor maid.

"Hello, Madame," she whispered, "so you're here too! Isn't it a swell party? Gee, how I'd like to be there myself."

A sudden thought struck me.

"Do you know everybody here?" I asked her.

She nodded as she answered proudly, "Sure I do, just point at any one over there and I'll tell you who it is."

"Well, who is that lady?" I asked, pointing at my little fairy as she floated by in her white and silver dress.

"That one? Oh, that's Mrs. Barr. Ain't she just beautiful, and she's that decent too. Always says, 'Good morning, Kathleen,' and 'good-by, Kathleen,' when she comes to our house and I open the door for her."

That information pleased me and with a warm glow of kindly feelings towards the diminutive Mrs. Barr who showed such decent feelings to poor little Irish door openers, I crawled out of the hedge and assuming a nonchalant air as though I had never been peeping through it, continued my walk ending up as usual at the House of Tears. That evening I sat there for a very long time, enjoying every minute of my precious freedom, while the hours sped pleasantly by. Stars, fire-flies, wide spaces and the sweet fragrance of wild flowers, all were there as usual to greet me and keep me company as long as I sat on my log. In some mysterious way it was in that spot, night after night, that I drew the necessary strength to carry on through those long and dreary days. It was as though I were a clock on legs that arrived there every evening ticking feebly and sorely in need of being wound up; in fact on the verge of stopping. And then just as I was about to peter out an unseen, powerful, Life-giving hand would wind me up again so effectively while I sat there that when it was time for me to go back to my room I'd feel full of vitality and energy and ready to endure another wearisome day.

One night I had a particularly interesting experience, that of seeing a meeting of the Ku Klux Klan. It happened this way:

One day at dinner in the boarding house the conversation became general about the Ku Klux Klan and a supposedly secret meeting that it was soon to hold somewhere nearby, though no one knew exactly when or where. To my surprise the gasoline tank driver, who up to this time had always kept very silent, devoting all his attention to food, suddenly became quite loquacious and seemed to know a great deal about the Klan, as he dropped mysterious hints with an air of secretive importance. Much interested and eager to hear some more about it, I went up to him after dinner and asked a few questions that he readily answered. Then when every one was arguing loudly about the Klan he suddenly whispered:

"Lookee here, Ma'am, if you really want to see a Klan meeting, be in Rider's field to-morrow night about eleven. And if any one notices you and asks you who you are, say that Charlie, the driver, sent you. And if they won't let you stay near the circle ask them to call me and I'll see that no one chases you away."

Amazed at such confidence in me, an utter stranger, I stammered my thanks and before he could change his mind hastily assured him that I would be there the following evening without fail. All next day I was in a fever of excitement, afraid that Mrs. Hipper would detain me until midnight and that I would miss the meeting. But luck was on my side and just before dinner Mrs. Hipper told me that she did not require my presence that evening as she was going out to play bridge. With a sigh of relief I scampered to the boarding house, swallowed my dinner as fast as I could and then immediately started out on my expedition to the meeting, having quite a long distance to go. But I walked so fast that at ten o'clock I had already reached the field, where despite the darkness I could distinguish a large crowd of strange, shapeless white figures. Coming closer I saw that they were dressed like ghosts in loose white garments with white cowls that entirely covered their heads and faces, leaving only narrow slits for their eyes. Besides being so ghost-like they reminded me too of the mysterious Brothers of Mercy that I had seen in the streets of Italy, either bearing the coffin of some one too poor to be buried in any other way, or else hurrying on some secret errand of mercy. And I was much interested when an Italian once told me that most of the Brothers belong to the greatest families in Italy and that the secrecy of their order was such that two friends, playing cards in the same club and at the same table, did not know they both belonged to the order of the Brothers of Mercy, and when summoned in the midst of their game to accomplish some duty— such as burying the dead or assisting the sick—never knew who the other Brother was, as the rules of the order forbade that they disclose their identity by word or sign.

Staring at the white figures of the Klansmen I wondered if by any chance their order was as much like the Italian one in spirit as it was in dress. At first there wasn't much to see except a large crowd of white figures milling around in a dark field; then suddenly things began to happen. First of all a squadron of mounted Klansmen appeared, bearing flaming torches and riding horses that seemed unnatural and gaunt as they also were swathed in white. As soon as they reached the outskirts of the field these riders stopped, and then breaking ranks, in single file formed a great circle that began slowly to move around in one direction. New Klansmen on foot were pouring in all the time from everywhere until it seemed to me that inside that weird circle thousands of white figures had assembled. Then automobiles arrived, bearing electric crosses that stood upright on their hoods, and aeroplanes, invisible but for those same crosses on their bodies, passed low over the field creating the amazing impression of shining crosses, flying in all directions unattached to anything material. By the light of the torches I could see that eight platforms had been erected inside the magic circle, while in its very center at the stroke of midnight three enormous crosses suddenly burst into flame like a fiery Golgotha.

"Onward Christian Soldiers," sang the multitude of white figures, and then the mysteries of their rites began. Though no one had noticed me I did not dare go up too close to the circle and breathlessly watched every move that was made. It must have been an initiation ceremony for a large number of men dressed in ordinary clothes were then brought into the circle and between two lines of Klansmen were taken from one platform to another, where an apparently important Klansman seemed to question each one in turn. This lasted for a long time, then finally, after they had all been brought up to each platform, they were given the same white garments as the Klansmen and white wooden crosses to carry. Then after a few more marchings and singings the ceremony ended. Aeroplanes and automobiles disappeared, the riders put out their torches and rode away, and the great multitude of Klansmen suddenly discarded their white robes and turned into a dark crowd of ordinary-looking people.

Breathless I ran back home, arriving at my room at three o'clock in the morning, too excited to sleep or even undress.

The only real pleasure I had those days was the arrival of letters from abroad, from London and Paris. All my friends seemed to understand how desperately lonely I was in Dawn and wrote frequently. Grand Duchess Xenia, Lady Carnock, the Archbishop Eulogius of Paris and many others wrote long letters describing all the news that they thought would interest me and tried their best to cheer me up. Twice a day the mailman, a stocky, pleasant little fellow would come trudging up Jackson avenue nearly always bringing something for me in his bag. He became so used to the number of letters that I received daily, that when it happened that he didn't have anything for me he'd be quite chagrined and would call out in a troubled voice:

"Can you beat it, Countess, there's nothing for you to-day!"

Sometimes when Mrs. Hipper went out in the evening I would walk down to the Wolf theater and there try to forget my tiresome life in the contemplation of some exciting movie. As far as pictures were concerned I got on very well, but when it came to vaudeville I felt utterly lost, as I couldn't understand the rapid speech of the comedians and therefore missed every single joke. And no matter how attentive I was nor how much I strained my ears and my mind, I would sit dismally nonplussed while the theater rocked with laughter. Even the captions of the funny pictures would leave me perplexed, anxiously trying to figure out where the joke was and usually failing miserably in the attempt. Once, however, when "ads" were being flashed onto the screen, I thought I saw a funny one and shrieked with laughter to show the audience that I had understood the point before any one else had. All it said was "Oswego," in large letters beneath the picture of some rather ordinary-looking buildings that might have belonged to any Mid-Western town. But I thought that "Oswego" was the humorous distortion of the words: "As we go" and laughed uproariously, not so much at the joke, which I didn't think was so very funny after all, but at the delight of having at last grasped the salt of pure American humor. But as I looked around me, in the way one does at the theater when everybody is enjoying the same thing together, I was surprised to see that no one was even smiling; on the contrary the farmer on my right was actually glaring at me angrily. Feeling that I had made a bad mistake somewhere I stopped laughing, composed my features and with a seriously attentive gaze watched "Oswego" fade off the screen. That evening as I walked home with Anna, the nurse, who had been to the movies too, I asked her what "Oswego" meant and felt extremely small and silly when she answered:

"Why, it's just the name of a town, Madame! . . . Didn't you see it advertised on the screen?"

The heat that summer was terrific and my room intolerable. There wasn't anything I could do about it, either, as my fellow boarder, Mr. Brooks, usually sat in his room opposite mine with his door wide open and not a stitch of clothes on (though he always wore his glasses), so that I had to keep my own door closed, while the unwelcome strains of the eternal "Banana" song obliged me to shut my window too. The only thing for me to do was to go out, and whenever I could I walked to the House of Tears and sat there until late.

After my first terrifying experience with the nocturnal freight train I became strangely attracted to it and would run every night to the same street crossing to watch it pass. No matter where I was, at Mrs. Hipper's or at my House of Tears or in the street, aimlessly walking for the sake of getting tired, I would become very restless shortly before midnight, when it was time for the ghost train to appear and if I was late would start running breathlessly so as to meet it at the corner. Usually I'd get there ahead of time and leaning against a certain tree, always the same one, would wait for the distant sounds that heralded the train's approach. The rusty tracks, unused except for that one midnight trip, lay in a straight line across the field, enabling me to see in the far distance the first faint glimmer of the locomotive's headlight and to hear the sinister clanging of its bell long before it arrived at the street crossing. If I came too early I would peer into the darkness, with beating heart and clammy hands, straining my eyes to catch the first gleam of light—not larger than a will o' the wisp—and listening intently for that far-off bell. As the train came nearer and nearer its strange fascinating power over me would become so great that the cold perspiration would break out all over my body and I'd tremble from head to foot. And every time the train passed the tree where I was leaning, with my arms thrown around it and fingers digging into its bark, I'd close my eyes so as not to see the great wheels slowly roll by. It terrified me and yet attracted me as a friend on whom I could rely without fail. I knew it would be there every night, I knew it could annihilate me whenever I wished it to do so and yet I felt that the final decision lay within me, therefore making me its master.

I was pretty desperate those days and on September 5th wrote in my Diary:

"I am just a machine that is alive in a mechanical way, that's all. And I am alive because I don't dare put an end to my life.

"I do not read any serious books because I cannot study. To study, to concentrate, to work mentally would be to live, and I must not live, I dare not live, for then I would think, and thoughts are too painful.

"I do not read any novels and easy books, for now they do not interest me. When I have read a few pages I always know how they will end and that makes me feel so old, so hopelessly old.

"I cannot sew, for then again my thoughts and re-membrances are my companions and I must not think, I must not remember.

"I do not care to walk, for I have nowhere to go except the House of Tears, and walk only because a hu-man machine must walk, my legs demand it, my whole body urges me on . . . so I go aimlessly along and re-turn only when I feel too tired to keep going.

"I do not care to drive—where should I go to? There is nothing to be seen here but fields, endless fields.

"I do not write for the same reason that I do not read:

if I wrote—I would be writing down my thoughts, and they would make me suffer.

"I eat, I sleep, I move, I teach—because I am alive and have to go through all these motions. But I am, oh, so tired! It is horrible not to have any one in the whole world—to be alone, alone, alone. Nothing to look forward to, no thoughts but those of the past that form a chain of sorrow that I try to forget, nothing in the present, nothing, nothing, nothing. Only the House of Tears and the Midnight train keep me alive, for they are the only things that I look forward to all day long.

"Oh, won't ever, ever anything good happen to me again?"

About that time I was ignominiously chased out of Mrs. Pance's boarding house. One day after dinner, as I was standing on her porch talking to old Mr. Holl, one of the railroad boys came up and offered me a cigarette saying:

"Surely, Frenchie, you enjoy a good smoke, and this brand is fine—I won the box yesterday."

Thanking him, I took a cigarette and lighted it when all of a sudden I heard a howl and wheeling around saw Mrs. Pance behind me, with crimson cheeks and popping eyes, staring at my cigarette in horror. For a few seconds she stood there speechless, the very picture of accusing fury . . . then giving vent to another howl she rushed towards me and shaking her fist in my face shouted:

"Throw that away, you wicked, sinful woman! Throw that away at once, and don't you dare do it again, hear me?"

Amazed I stared at her, while Mr. Holl murmured soothingly:

"Now, now, Mrs. Pance, don't get so upset, it's all right—she didn't know that you didn't like ladies to smoke here."

But Mrs. Pance would not be appeased, and continued to advance towards me threateningly until she came up quite close. For a second I thought she meant to hit me, and everybody else on the porch must have had that same thought, for there was a dead silence, and not a person moved. "What does one do in a case like this, strike back?" I had time to wonder. But then, just as the situation was becoming unbearable, Mr. Duty sneezed loudly and the tension snapped. Some one laughed, the figures on the porch began to stir naturally, Mr. Holl came between me and Mrs. Pance and taking hold of her fat arm quietly led her away indoors. As for me, quivering with indignation and anger, I ran down the steps, tore down the street and into the Hippers' house, rushing into their library in a state of boiling rage. Mrs. Hipper was lying on her sofa asleep but I didn't care.

"That woman has insulted me and I'll never go back there again," I cried, grabbing her by the shoulder, and shaking her into a sitting posture while she blinked at me incomprehendingly.

"Who did what and where?" she finally asked, looking so funny I would have laughed had I not been so angry.

"The Pance woman shouted at me insultingly and nearly hit me because I smoked a cigarette on her porch after dinner," I explained a little more coherently, but she merely shrugged her shoulders and remarked in her mealy way that that was my business and not hers.

"Oh, yes, it is your business," I retorted, beginning to boil over again, "I am an utter stranger here, I came to work for you, you made me eat in that horrible boarding house, and now I tell you I'll never go back there again—never! I'd rather starve. . . ."

At last Mrs. Hipper grasped the situation.

"Oh, wee," she said, getting off the sofa, putting on her glasses, and shaking out the folds of her dress. "Oh, wee, I see now, I see. She objected to you smoking a cigarette, was that it? Answer me in French."

"Objected nothing, and I'll speak English," I cried quite rudely, "I tell you she shouted at me and shook her fist and nearly hit me, and I won't go back, and if you say that I must—I'll leave you right now, contract

[213]

or no contract, and seek protection at the British Consulate!"

This speech produced the desired effect. Mrs. Hipper looked alarmed, stared at me as though she were seeing me for the first time and after a moment's silence declared:

"All right, you don't have to go back and you may have all your meals here with Anna and the children; I'll tell the cook."

"I don't care where I eat," I answered, "as long as I never see that Bella Vista of the Pance again."

And so a change for the better was effected in my life. I never returned to the boarding house, and had my meals with Anna and the children, while Mrs. Hipper had hers in solitary grandeur in the dining room.

In October, however, she astounded me one day by sending me an engraved invitation that requested the presence of "The Countess" at the Hippers' residence at a certain date for dinner. As she had not said anything to me about it, though as usual I saw her every day from eight o'clock in the morning until midnight, I could hardly believe my own eyes, and taking the invitation along with me, asked her what it meant.

"Just what it says," she replied with a freezing look. "And besides isn't there R. S. V. P. at the bottom? You surely should know what that means!"

"Why, yes," I murmured dubiously, still staring at

the card with unbelieving eyes, "I know, and I'll come of course if you wish me to."

"Is that the way to accept a formal invitation?" she inquired, now quite peeved. "Don't you think you should answer in the proper fashion according to etiquette?"

"All right, I will," I agreed, stifling a wild desire to laugh, and then, for some inexplicable reason, thinking once more of "Alice in Wonderland," and of the part where the Dodo after the race presents her solemnly with her own thimble. "This is just as nonsensical," I thought, but after the unfortunate story of Themistocles, having learned to control my features, I bowed gravely and answered that I would be pleased to send in my formal acceptance that very evening. Which I did.

When the day of the dinner party arrived I was told to put on my black silk evening dress and to appear at exactly half past seven. My surprise cannot be described when on entering the front door (I had also been told to be sure and come in that way and not through the kitchen as usual) Mrs. Hipper suddenly advanced towards me with outstretched hands exclaiming effusively:

"Why, Countess, this is a pleasure indeed!" And then introduced me to all her guests. Every one called me Countess, every one beamed on me, and as a climax that I would never have believed possible, I was seated on

Mr. Hipper's right. It was then that I had my first real talk with him and found him quite entertaining. But all through dinner I could not understand what had happened and why I had been admitted to the table, when all of a sudden an inadverent word of Mr. Hipper's explained the riddle: the guests were all "out of town guests" from New York and Washington, and I, with my title, was playing the rôle of Tchekov's "poor General" who used to be hired for parties so as to impress newcomers with his high rank and decorations. That discovery "finished" me and I burst out laughing, and laughed all evening long. Luckily Mr. Hipper was telling funny stories so that I could laugh without disgracing myself and Mrs. Hipper continued to beam on me as I heard her remark to one of the guests that the dear little Countess was the very soul of merriment and fun!

All went off splendidly as far as I was concerned, and after that whenever out of town guests arrived I used to be formally invited to dinner and greeted effusively at the front door with welcoming cries and outstretched hands. I learned my rôle perfectly and only regretted that Tchekov was not there to see me play it.

That winter, whenever the Hippers went to Metropole to the opera, I used to accompany them, and the next day would be described in the newspapers as their charming guest of honor.

At Christmas I had a shock. According to Russian custom, having bought presents for the entire Hipper household, I was worried when it came to getting something for Mrs. Hipper, for I thought that I could not possibly give her anything like, for instance, a bottle of perfume, or a pair of silk stockings, and finally decided to present her with one of my own beloved possessions that Dr. Golder had brought out of Russia for me. After much grave deliberation my choice fell on an antique Eighteenth Century French fan, beautifully hand-painted and mounted on a mother-of-pearl holder, richly carved and embossed with gold. The fan was signed with the name of the famous artist who had painted it. It had belonged to my great grandmother and was considered by connoisseurs to be a very lovely and valuable object. So on Christmas morning I wrapped it up carefully and with many precautions, as the pavements were dangerously slippery, carried it to Mrs. Hipper's house. There, chuckling at the thought of her delight, I sat in the hall waiting for her to come down and turn on the electric lights on the Christmas tree before she summoned the children. I was so excited at the thought of giving her something really lovely that I could hardly keep still, and catching a glimpse of myself in the mirror saw that my cheeks were flaming red and my eyes shining. For the first time since I had come to Dawn I felt happy, in that indescribable "Christmas" frame of mind. Surrounded by the presents that I had bought for the children and the servants, I sat holding the fan on my lap, and impatiently watching the clock. At last as it struck eight I heard a door open upstairs, followed by the appearance of Mrs. Hipper looking very sleepy and disheveled as she came down the steps in trailing early morning draperies. Seeing me submerged beneath my packages she stopped and stared.

"What on earth have you got there?" she asked, while I answered delightedly: "Presents for everybody."

"Presents? But you shouldn't have done that," she exclaimed disapprovingly. "Why, I never give anybody anything but money. Only Mr. Hipper and the children receive gifts from me."

With a slight chill at heart and a sense of foreboding I got up and collecting my various parcels followed her into the picture gallery where in a corner stood the tree. There were no little tables laden with gifts around it, as we always had in Russia, and, but for the children's toys scattered beneath the lower boughs, the room looked dreary and bare in the bleak wintry morning light. Putting my packages down on an armchair I helped Mrs. Hipper turn on the gayly colored electric bulbs, and then at her request went upstairs to tell Anna that she might bring the children down. The next minute they came rushing in, and, after the first exclamation of delight at seeing the glittering tree, threw themselves on the toys and with little joyous shrieks began to look over their presents. Then Mrs. Hipper told Anna to call in the servants, and, while she was gone, turned to me saying:

"When they come I want you to go outside in the hall and then lead them in. After all you come first, you know."

Mechanically I obeyed, and with leaden footsteps went into the hall where already the servants had assembled and a line was being formed. Once again I caught a glimpse of my face in the same mirror and saw that now I had turned a ghastly white while my eyes stared back at me dull and lustreless. Anna was busily lining every one up according to rank and when ready wound up the victrola, started a march, clapped her hands three times and cried out:

"Now, Madame, lead them on!"

"Here goes the poor hired General with his decorations again," I thought, as in a dream I advanced, and entering the picture gallery once more, was the first to receive a large gayly colored paper hat box from Mrs. Hipper's hands. On a table next to her were piled a lot of similar hat boxes evidently destined to be distributed among my followers. Standing aside to allow the others to approach I opened the box and finding in it a package done up in tissue paper began to unwrap it. Layer after layer came off and yet I couldn't find anything. At last after accumulating a mountain of discarded tissue-paper on the floor at my feet, I came to a small envelope tied with a red ribbon and opening it found a ten-dollar gold piece. For a minute I stared at it unbelievingly, then without saying a word, gave Mrs. Hipper the little box containing the precious fan, and with trembling knees walked out of the room leaving all the other gifts that I had bought for the servants lying on the chair where I had deposited them. Down Jackson avenue I stumbled to the house where I lived and up the stairs to my room. There, locking the door I threw myself on the floor, and, unable to cry, beat it with my fists until the acute physical pain in them overcame the mental hurt. Then too desperate and sick to be able to pull myself together I lowered the window-shades, and creeping into bed remained there all that day. When Mrs. Whopple knocked at the door and asked me what was the matter, I replied that I had a bad headache and requested her to telephone Mrs. Hipper and tell her that I would not be able to read to her that afternoon. In the evening I got up and as usual went to the House of Tears where I remained until day-break. At midnight I heard in the distance the ghost train passing over the rusty rails that seemed to shriek in agony as it came over the fields to the street crossing, while its bell sounded more sinister than ever. And though when I heard the first clanging of that bell I knew that if I ran I'd meet the train at the crossing, I realized full well that this time it would master me, and clinging desperately to the log that was the House of Tears, stayed there all night long.

A few days later Mrs. Hipper had a caller—a social worker soliciting money. Of course I was present when she came, reading Dumas as usual, and sat quietly by listening to what she had to say. But when she finished and Mrs. Hipper was preparing to write out a check I spoke up and said that I too wanted to contribute my share. Then, despite Mrs. Hipper's protests, in the queer language she called French and that only I in the whole world understood, I ran "home" and finding the famous Christmas ten-dollar gold piece that had caused me so much grief, returned to the Hipper house and presented the coin to the social worker. Mrs. Hipper peered at me in surprise then remarked reprovingly:

"Why, it's your Christmas gold piece! You shouldn't give away such large sums of money to charity."

It was then that I understood that she had not meant to hurt me when she gave me the ten dollars, as to all the servants, and that her point of view was, and always would be that of some one who could never get used to the fact of having suddenly become rich. After that I liked her better and instead of being angered or hurt by her sayings and doings, felt only amused and sorry.

That winter was unusually long and dreary, and the days dragged by with feet of lead. Dumas from morning 'til night was beginning to tell on me and I became positively hungry for books of another kind. As it became too cold to sit for any length of time in the House of Tears, and besides there wasn't much to see there as the fire-flies had disappeared long ago and the stars were rarely visible—after my evening walk I would return to my room and then read in bed for hours. The very first book that fell into my hands was Sinclair Lewis's *Main Street*, and I cannot adequately describe my amazement at reading such an accurate and true portrayal of a town so much like *Dawn*. His descriptions of the streets, houses, people and customs were so powerful and so vivid that at times it seemed uncanny. Why should I be reading such a book when I was actually living the life he spoke of and in a way gradually becoming one of his characters? The coincidence was too remarkable and as I read on my eyes grew rounder and rounder and I would devour the pages as fast as my mind permitted. It was one of those strange things that can never be explained, as, for instance, thinking of a certain person that one believes to be far away and then unexpectedly running into that person on the street; or else, when a certain word or tune keeps going through one's mind, to hear somebody say that word or hum that tune aloud. Many times it has happened to me, as it has prob-

ably to every one else, that during a pause in a conversation I'll think: "Now, so and so is going to say that
word." And then I stare at him (or her) anxiously, even
fearfully, as though my life depended on hearing that
word, and, to my immense relief, I hear it!

Mysterious undercurrents—puzzling, fascinating and
bewildering—that make one feel like a helpless child
who is being directed to act a certain way, speak a certain way and walk down a certain path of life.

The coincidence of reading that book at a time when
I, a foreigner, was seeing Main Street with my own eyes
and living its life, impressed me so strongly that I immediately classified it as one of the greatest books I had
ever read and I have never changed my mind since.

However I was foolish enough to express my opinion
to Mrs. Hipper who grew very angry, and said
that Sinclair Lewis didn't know what he was writing
about, just as I hadn't the slightest idea of what I was
saying. As it was no use arguing with her I dropped the
subject though she often referred to it and tried to
point out to me how very mistaken I was.

The inhabitants of Dawn were none too friendly towards me and treated me with suspicion.

"Well, she may have been a countess over there,
though I doubt that very much, she certainly doesn't
dress like one now," I heard my landlady say once to
some of her friends just as I was entering the house.

And that seemed to be the general attitude towards me. Everywhere I went, whether walking down the streets or entering a store or meeting some one either at Mrs. Hipper's or Mrs. Whopple's house, I was looked over very carefully with eyes that expressed more curiosity and hostility than anything else, while the half-amused, half-disdainful smiles seemed to say: "You can't put anything over on us here, we know that you're only an impostor!"

It would have been very easy for Mrs. Hipper to dispel those suspicions as she knew exactly who I was, having had plenty of references about me in London. But for some reason she never spoke in my defense and the unfriendly attitude persisted during the entire year of my life in Dawn. It came to the point where I hated walking down the streets in the day-time because I knew that I was being surreptitiously watched from many windows, and that every move I made was noticed and then commented upon. Whether they thought that I was a militant anarchist carrying a bomb in my pocket or whether they were afraid that I might break into their homes and steal all that I could lay my hands on, I don't know to this day. But that atmosphere of constant hostility and suspicion made me feel like a hunted animal, and filled me with fear. Then too, Anna, the children's nurse, used to tell me choice bits of gossip— mostly what people said about me, and as they never said anything kind, that only made matters worse.

"Oh, Madame," she would say, usually at meal time, "you'll split your sides with laughter when I tell you what Mrs. Jones said about you to Mrs. Brown. I overheard her in the drug-store where I was getting some of that new rouge (and, by the way, you really should try it—it's awfully good, and a little touch of it on your cheeks would work wonders. Really if only you'd let me make you up a bit you'd look like a different person). Well, anyway, as I was saying, I heard Mrs. Jones say to Mrs. Brown: 'That countess' (and here they both started to laugh and laugh as though you weren't a countess at all!) 'that countess goes past my house every evening, walking slowly with her head down as if she didn't see anything but the sidewalk. And do you know where she goes? To the end of Jackson avenue where she sits on that dirty old log for hours. We followed her several times and watched her sit there with her shoulders bent and her shabby old coat all humped up. We just laughed so hard watching her we were afraid she'd hear us. And there she sits and sits. We thought maybe she was waiting for some man, but no, no man ever comes . . . Well, as the saying goes—a count is of no account—and there's no accounting what this countess will do.' Well, Madame, they laughed again, then suddenly noticed me and stopped talking, but I thought I'd tell you to make you laugh too."

And so the winter months crept on,—hostile, dreary, endless. In March, however, two events occurred that brought some pleasant changes in my life.

One evening when I came home to Mrs. Whopple's house I met in the corridor a stranger—a young man who threw me a searching look, bowed slightly, and then went into the room opposite mine. As Mr. Brooks had left us in the Fall and I knew that Mrs. Whopple was advertising for a new roomer I decided that this was he, and then forgot all about him. Up in the morning at seven and home late at night I hardly ever saw any one of the Whopple household except once in a while the eldest daughter May, who would be just going out with her beau. But I heard from her that we had a new roomer, that he had been in the Navy, was a graduate of Annapolis, very good-looking (*that* I had seen during the brief moment of our encounter) and a very delightful person, though "somewhat high-hat and happy-go-lucky, the usual Navy combination," she said and asked me if I'd like to meet him. I said I didn't care either way, as I had no time for men, no matter how good-looking and charming and promptly forgot him again. Two or three weeks must have passed since his arrival, when one evening, as I was sitting in the Whopples' living room playing the piano (Mrs. Hipper having gone to Metropole) I heard some one come in the room, and turning around on my piano stool saw that it

[226]

was the Navy man. He looked so nice and clean, as if he had mysteriously just had a dip in the sea, and so absolutely different from anybody else that I had seen in Dawn, that I felt immediately attracted to him, and answered his greetings with a smile as friendly as his. All that evening we sat and talked. He told me that his family lived in Cambridge, Massachusetts—that he loved the East, was desperately homesick for it and wanted to go back as soon as he could; that he had just been retired from the Navy on account of ill health, and was heartbroken because he could not return to active service.

"It's all right to be honorably retired with a pension as I am when one is old," he said, "but at my age it's pretty awful and I don't know how I'll ever get used to the fact that I am 'out' and a civilian for life."

He had come to Dawn to study business conditions in the Middle West and had purposely chosen Dawn in order to get away from the sea as far as possible and be in an environment as totally different from his old one as could be. He also told me about his older brother Edward, who had been a Commander in the Navy, aide to Admiral Sims, and had received the Distinguished Service Medal for handling all communications between America and her Allies during the World War. He died "over there" and after his death his name was entered in the Gold Star Record of Massachusetts, and a street in Cambridge was named after him.

And the longer we sat and talked the more I liked him, and when finally we said good-night I realized that I had met at last some one who "spoke my language," looked at life very much the way I did and apparently was a kindred spirit. After that we became great friends, and were together as often as we could be. Sometimes when the Whopple living room was unoccupied we would sit there and talk, or else we'd go for a walk, though he couldn't walk very much in those days on account of his recent illness, or we'd go to the movies. It was there that we ran into Mr. Duty once who looked at me reproachfully and sadly said:

"So you *have* a gentleman friend after all! . . ."

And at that same time in March I had an unexpected caller—Lyta Barr. She came in one evening bringing me a large bunch of white flowers and invited me to dinner the following night. Intelligent, kindly, understanding, she saw the difficult situation that I was in, and from that memorable evening did everything in her power to brighten my life and make things a little pleasanter. For instance she would take me driving whenever I could go, which of course wasn't very often but was something for me to look forward to, and sent me books and flowers and asked me often to her house, where as we say in Russian: "I used to rest my soul."

Thus with my two new friends life became much easier. But when my year in Dawn was nearly over and Mrs. Hipper one evening started talking about renewing my contract for another twelve months, my heart sank in despair. Renew that awful contract and deliberately enter a second year of Dumas and dreariness—it was more than I could face! That night I sat for hours in the House of Tears weighing the pros and cons of the situation, the only pros of remaining with the Hippers being that if I left them I would find myself without work in a strange country and with no money to tide over the period when I'd be unemployed. Of course I knew that I could write to my old American friends and ask them to help me to find something to do, but I hated asking anybody for anything, infinitely preferring to fight my own way alone without assistance.

Slowly I walked to my new room in a Mrs. Thinpet's house (Mrs. Whopple had sold her home that was too large for her and moved into a smaller one where there was no place for me). Getting into bed I lay staring into the darkness as I tried to solve my problem. Hour after hour passed and I couldn't sleep as I tossed and twisted and turned, while visions of another dismal year in Dawn floated through my mind. Then, just as I was going to get up and dress, having abandoned all hope of sleep, I suddenly remembered that a couple of months previously, when I had had trouble with my throat as a result of reading too much aloud, the doctor had given me a small box of sleeping tablets that I had never even opened. Turning on the light and finding the box in my suitcase where I had carelessly thrust it, I tore it open and taking it back to bed with me picked out one of the tablets and swallowed it. But it didn't make me sleepy so presently I took another one, and as that didn't seem to have any effect, soon reached for a third. That one must have doped and dazed me to the extent that I didn't realize what I was doing, for (as I was told later) I had swallowed all the tablets in that box with the result that next morning I was found in my bed unconscious and dying. Rushed to the hospital in an ambulance I lay at death's door for nearly a week. Then slowly I began to recover to the surprise of the doctors who had not expected me to live, as those innocent-looking sleeping tablets had turned out to be nothing less than veronal! Why any doctor should have given them to me without warning and why such a tremendous dose had not killed me, will always be a mystery. But again to quote an old Russian saying: "There is no evil without good" and in this particular case the "good" proved to be the peace and quiet of my hospital room, where I had time to think and to make decisions without any hurry. It was there that I definitely made up my mind not to return to the Hippers and wrote them a letter to that effect, and never saw them again. That done I felt immensely relieved, and though poverty and the unknown stared me once more in the face I was happy to be free. According to the contract the Hippers were to give me a sum of money that would pay my way back to England, but I decided that I could use it in America instead where it would help me live for a while. So not knowing what to do or where to go after I left the hospital I took a tiny apartment in Dawn and, using that as my headquarters, began to look for work. The street I lived on was called Locust, but having received a letter from a Russian that was amazingly addressed to "Grasshopper Street" and that had actually reached me—I rechristened my street "Grasshopper" and Grasshopper it was to the end. My apartment (really nothing but one room with a bathroom and kitchenette) was a nice little place and I became greatly attached to it, to such an extent that when I found work in Metropole I went on living in Dawn and commuted every day. During those months I saw a great deal of my two friends, mostly in the evenings and our three-cornered friendship became one of the most delightful I ever experienced. Only when they both left Dawn, she for a winter in the South, he back to the East, and when I became very tired commuting, did I finally decide to give up my apartment and move to Metropole to the Sidewater Hotel.

My first work in Metropole was in the Real Estate business. A friend of some of my old friends in England had casually suggested at lunch one day that I try it out, and I promptly decided to do so though I hadn't the slightest idea what the work would be. The very words "Real Estate" were most puzzling. And why "real" I could never quite understand.

Every morning early I'd drive down from the Sidewater Hotel to the office on top of the bus and arrive in time for the lecture that was delivered daily by our sales manager, a very energetic man who would talk appealingly and in colorful terms about the most hideous parts of the town.

"Drive your prospective buyer to the new development on the west side and tell him how beautiful it will be in ten years," he would cry, pounding the table with his fists and mopping his forehead and loosening his collar in a frenzy of selling enthusiasm, while I would listen and wonder how on earth I could describe in glowing terms the future beauty of a place which to me looked like the most God-forsaken spot on earth. However I tried my best and even took a 'prospective buyer' down there, where in a faltering voice and under a pouring rain I began to praise the marvelous possibilities of that dismal swampy division. All I had to boast about was a large, flat, mud-covered area with cement sidewalks surprisingly laid out in symmetrical lines all over it, and drooping little red flags which under the steady downpour flopped drearily against their sticks, while the wind in fitful gusts brought an overpowering odor from the stockyards.

"Here will be your house—a model of convenience and luxury," I went on as I delivered my professional sales talk number 4, which I thought would be the most appropriate in this particular case, and trying to smile brightly and convincingly though more than anything I wanted to pull out my handkerchief and hold it up to my nose while I talked. My "buyer" must have felt the same way, for he sniffed several times disapprovingly and then remarked coldly:

"And how about that abominable stench? Will it always be here, and if so what does your company propose to do about it?"

"Oh, that little drawback depends entirely the way the wind blows, you'll hardly ever notice it," I answered persuasively. But at that moment a fresh gust of wind brought us such a powerful whiff of stockyard, that we both choked, coughed and then without another word turned towards the car, climbed into it and drove back to the city in silence.

"Well, and how did you make out?" asked the sales manager when, dripping and crestfallen, I came into the office. Then, when he had heard my dismal story, he delivered a private lecture for my sole benefit and told me exactly why I had failed. "You should have diverted his attention," he cried. "You should have used your feminine wiles and made him forget all about the smell! That's why we like to send out attractive young women with difficult masculine prospects, for they can do so much that way." At this point he smiled sweetly, winked one eye, and twisting his body into an extraordinary pose, pitched his voice into a thin, high key: "Oh, Mr. Jones" . . . (you should say) "oh, you're just too nice for words . . . See what a dandy little home you'll have here, a love nest . . . oh, it will be so sweet" (and the sales manager sighed ecstatically and, wiggling himself around like a contortionist, looked at me with what was supposed to be a very bewitching feminine smile). "There," he then remarked in his natural voice, "that's the way you should do it . . . Sales talk number 4 indeed—you'll never get anywhere that way. Why we always send the good-looking young men of our force with the ladies, and, boy, how they work. You know Simpson, don't you? Well, he's rich now and all through selling to the ladies. Ask him how he does it!" And with a chuckle the manager moved away.

"Never mind, don't worry, you'll get there some day," whispered a voice in my ear, and the next minute a tall, heavy man with a kindly face introduced himself gravely, saying: "My name is MacUren and I'm very pleased to meet you." He bowed politely and proffered his big soft hand.

"Delighted," I murmured as I shook hands with him and then sat down wearily on the chair that he had pulled out for me. I had really worked hard that day and my failure was making me feel wretched.

"Look here, I'll cheer you up," said Mr. MacUren encouragingly, "I've been watching you for some time and think that you're fine in every way—honest. Now how about our going over those sales lists of yours together? You see I'm an old hand at this game and can give you a pointer or two that may help you a lot. Come on, smile now and tell your uncle MacUren all about your real estate troubles (the others you'll tell me when we get better acquainted). Well, shall we work on those lists together?"

"All right, to-morrow morning I'll show them to you, but to-day I'm too tired," I answered gravely, as I didn't much care for his jocular tone and "uncle Mac-Uren" seemed to be the last drop in an overflowing cup. Then I went home to the Sidewater Hotel and from my window watched the day wane as the sun set in a riot of red and gold that played over the water for a long while. Then the red and gold faded, the water became gray, darkness fell, and all I could see was a vast black dome studded with stars.

The next morning I kept my promise and showed the

lists to Mr. MacUren but it proved to be an unwise move, for shortly afterwards he proposed to me saying that if I consented to marry him he would even be willing to change his somewhat cumbersome name of MacUren to the lighter one of MacBride.

About a month after I joined the Real Estate business a big party was given for the Sales Force. After a copious and noisy dinner at the Duck Hotel we sallied forth down the principal thoroughfare, as many as could crowd on the sidewalk abreast, arm in arm (I was held so firmly that I couldn't escape), with wreaths of flowers around our necks, loudly singing to the tune of Auld Lang Syne: "We're here because we're here, because we're here, because we're here . . ." Then all of a sudden the song would be broken off and the cheer leader, who also carried a large blue banner bearing the name of our firm in letters of gold, would yell vociferously:

"What is the matter with So and So?"

Whereupon the entire Sales Force would yell back in chorus:

"He's all right!"

"Who's all right?"

"So and So is all right!"

At last under pretext of having a bad headache I managed to wrench myself free and once more rushed back as fast as the bus could carry me, to the peace and quiet of my room at the hotel.

That room was really a delightful place and the evenings that I spent sitting on the sill of the wide bay window overlooking the water, were absolutely happy. Though I had no telescope I would star gaze for hours, watching the various constellations and trying to remember all that my amateur astronomical studies had taught me in my childhood. And while I sat in the dark room listening to the gentle swish swish of the water below, I would involuntarily be carried back again to the past and to the days when in Troitskoe I used to spend evening after evening with the big bronze telescope. Usually when it was warm I brought that telescope out on to the balcony where I had a good view of the sky, though the horizon was somewhat cut off by the tall trees of the park. Then, when it was too cold to be on the balcony, I would open the window in my old night nursery where I slept until my marriage, and, placing the telescope on the sill, I would content myself with gazing at only one side of the sky. How I loved that old nursery! Nothing ever changed in it and always the same old toys and things stood in their accustomed places: the big doll house with its four rooms, my favorite doll Esmeralda in her rose-colored bed, the white cupboard with glass doors filled with my childhood books and the pictures on the wall, cut out of some antiquated English magazine by my nurse long before I was born. There was a spell about that room that seemed to become stronger and stronger as I grew up and that held me to it with an unchangeable feeling of half-happiness, half-sadness. I never could define where one feeling ended and the other began, for they were curiously interwoven and often, in my happiest moments, my heart would suddenly contract with pain. But that pain would be of the kind that we call in Russian "a sweet pain" and was probably due to our racial temperament that is naturally streaked with veins of inexplicable sadness. But the best hours undoubtedly were those spent kneeling by the window, when I would turn the telescope on to the moon coming out slowly from behind the tree tops, which for a few moments would be silhouetted against the great silver disc in intricate patterns that looked like black lace. Then as the moon rose higher the lace work would gradually be transformed into long pointed fingers that seemed to have the power of holding her back for a short space of time while I fancied that I could see her grin widely and wink at me jovially as she calmly freed herself from their clutches and sailed up into the clear sky.

"The sea of tranquillity, the ocean of Tempests, the gulf of Irises, the great Crater of Copernic," I would whisper in awe as I turned my telescope on those favorite spots of mine with a proud feeling of possession. It was then that I composed lunar poems mostly in French which I wrote down feverishly in the silvery light that inspired them. Then I'd look around my nursery half flooded with the rays of the moon, half hidden in deep black shadows that seemed unreal and even terrifying, and—though I knew quite well that in that dark corner stood the familiar doll house, while in the other Esmeralda slept peacefully—I felt that the darkness concealed a world that had nothing to do with my toys and in which lurked all the mysterious beings that peopled the boundless and shadowy realm of the Unknown. When the moonlight would finally reach those corners and bring them back to life again I would heave a great sigh of relief and return to my telescope. After the moon, Jupiter was my favorite planet and when in a gayly colored Christmas fire-cracker I once found, hidden in the folds of a pink fool's-cap, a tiny slip of paper that said that Jupiter was the planet under which I had been born, I was deeply impressed and have firmly believed it ever since. Saturn came next, and the first time I found his rings I actually wept with joy.

And while I sat in my room of the Sidewater Hotel after a long "real estate" day those visions would crowd around me and I could see so clearly the old night nursery with its three windows framed with soft chintz curtains, my little mahogany bedstead in which probably many generations of Skariatine children had slept, my wash-stand with its blue and gold basins and jugs of all sizes, my toys, my books, my telescope and the form of a kneeling child gazing spellbound at the stars and dreaming strange dreams. I even fancied I could detect the strong perfume of the flowers beneath the nursery window about which I was dreaming and hear the soft song of the nightingale or the distant barking of a dog . . . Then the visions would float away and I'd find myself with many years between me and those days, but still staring out at the same unchangeable sky. Sometimes the past would float back again and other scenes would pass before me in slow procession all night long, one in particular recurring oftener than the others:

It is an early autumn day in the country, when the sun is hot, and the shade a trifle too cool, and the sky very blue, and the light very golden and the shadows sharp and black. We all sit in low wicker arm chairs beneath the old oak tree, where it smells strongly of violets though there are none in bloom. And there we read and write and talk in low tones to each other so as not to disturb the great silence around us. Softly my mother speaks of the books she is reading: sometimes it is Tagore, sometimes Adelaide Procter, sometimes a new writer of whom I have never heard. I sit a little apart from every one, mostly with my writing pad on my knees trying to express my thoughts and feelings. Diaries, sketches, poems—they pour helter skelter from my hard-working pencil—childish and pathetic. I am so anxious to write down what I think and feel and while

I am writing my mood is exalted, triumphant. Then I read over what I have written and realize with a shock that I have not expressed what I wanted to. Suddenly the leaves on the old oak tree begin to rustle and a cool wind cuts through the warmth that we're basking in.

"It's getting cold," my mother says, and orders me into the house until tea time. I love that hour too! The great dining room with its dark oak panels and green marble fireplace, the long table bearing the shining samovar, the multitudes of cups and glasses, the cakes and all kinds of good things to eat, the family and guests collecting from all over the place, and the talk that interests me so much because every one has something special to say. My father speaks about the peasants, the crops, the horses; my mother, about her garden, her books, her various plans, for she is always planning something new and to me delightful; the professor, about politics; my brother about his dogs and hunting, while next to me my governess gently murmurs something about her beloved Alsace Lorraine where she comes from and the town of her birth, Nancy. And all these waves of talk advance, recede, intermingle and heave around me like foam-crested breakers. Once in a while the speakers pause to listen politely to each other, but only for a brief moment. Then they continue their monologues, absorbed in their own thoughts, dreaming aloud and happy as the hot tea makes them comfortably warm and the sweet cakes smooth away all edges. And I think of the old Saint who recommended eating sweets whenever one feels mentally bitter or sour, and I look at all the kind, lovely people seated around the table and feel so happy that suddenly I laugh aloud.

"What are you laughing about, Miss Hahatounia?" asks the professor severely but with twinkling eyes and: "What's the matter, why 'the empty laughter of the fool,' Monkeyish Monkey?" asks my brother, trying to kick me under the table.

"Nothing," I answer, still laughing, "nothing at all, only everybody is so nice here, so nice that I just have to laugh! . . ."

But again the vision floats away and another one replaces it.

It is late autumn and the morning sun barely warms one. The courtyard is full of riding horses, their beautiful glossy coats gleaming, their saddles creaking, while their impatient hoofs paw the ground. The grooms have a hard time holding them and glance anxiously towards the door, hoping that the riders will soon come out. First my brother appears in riding coat and breeches and high spurred boots and a huntsman's horn slung around his side. He looks healthy and ruddy though very serious for a hunt is no joke with him. Then all the others come crowding out and they mount their horses and gravely ride away, each leading a pair of great borzoi dogs on long leashes. They have a big day ahead of them for they are going to hunt hares and foxes and wolves. As I hate seeing animals hunted and deliberately frighten them away from the huntsmen whenever I can, I'm left at home and then later on driven down with my mother to the hunt breakfast. A long table stands in a sheltered glade, with chairs and rugs all around it. The cook and his helpers, the butler and other servants are bustling about as they get things ready. The smoky smell of food being cooked out of doors over a crackling bonfire; the snorting of the horses somewhere not far off though they cannot be seen; the occasional growls of the borzois; the loud talk of the huntsmen and in the distance their trophies: the gaunt gray-haired wolves, the golden foxes and the silver hares, funny-looking even when they're dead—laid out on the grass or slung up on poles that make one think of a butcher's shop. And above it all, framed in the light blue sky, the pale sun of late autumn.

And yet another vision appears, a painful one this time, that hurts with sharp little stabs of agony, even though it all happened years ago.

I am in Troitskoe, in my old nursery, no longer a child but a very young married woman with two babies of my own. The smaller one, my little girl Maia, is asleep on my lap. Wrapped in a woolly pink blanket, with her round pink cheeks and soft, golden hair, she looks like a doll. "Shooinky" I call her for she loves my story about the imaginary birds that I "shoo" away by clapping my hands. She listens always so attentively and gravely until I reach the fascinating word "shoo"; then she gurgles and laughs delightedly while I hug her tight and whisper in her ear:

"Oh, Shooinky, you are my very own little bird, Shooinky."

On the floor at my feet my little boy is playing. Everybody still calls him Baby, but my name for him is Gingo, because Kipling's story of "Yellow Dog Dingo" is his favorite one and I have to tell it over and over again.

"Still ran Dingo, yellow Dog Dingo, always faster, always running faster, grinning like a horse collar," I murmur absent-mindedly while he watches my lips and gravely repeats the words after me. Only he says "Gingo" instead of Dingo and that is what I call him too.

His nurse thoroughly disapproves of that name and rebukes me every time I say it. "The very idea of calling the blessed angel a dog and a yellow dog at that," she grumbles. But he and I, we understand what it means; it is our own little joke, our secret, and we love it.

Suddenly I notice that his cheeks are flushed, and his blue eyes, usually so bright and starry, just like "star sapphires," are dark and heavy. Quickly I put the sleeping baby in her crib and then lift Gingo onto my lap.

"What's the matter, darling, are you ill?" I ask him anxiously as I put my hand on his forehead. It is hot, burning hot, and then I know that I have a very sick baby in my arms. I am stunned. It all came so quickly! Only a few minutes ago he was all right, laughing and playing in the pink of health. Now, all of a sudden, he is stricken. But something has to be done, quick. With shaking hands I put him to bed, then I telegraph the doctor who is eighty miles away (for the first time we have no doctor in the house); I carry all the unnecessary furniture out of the room, for I have a terrifying premonition that this is going to be no ordinary sickness; I lower the shades and then I settle down in my nurse's old arm chair next to his crib, the very same crib I used to sleep in as a baby, and begin the most agonizing vigil of all vigils in this world, that of a mother at her dying child's bed-side. Three days and three nights of nightmare followed. The doctor arrives and departs saying that there is no danger, nothing to worry about. Then he returns again and declares it is diphtheria . . . serum is needed at once, but he has none with him. A special messenger is sent post-haste back to the town of Orel, eighty miles away, to fetch the serum, but what with the muddy roads of November and trains that do not run often it takes him twelve hours to go there and back. Finally he brings the serum just ten minutes before the baby dies. Anguish upon anguish, those three days and nights are filled with hours and minutes of sheer anguish. My father tip-toes heavily in and out of the nursery, bringing every time something sacred to save his little grandson. First it is an Icon that he reveres very highly, then a miracle-working Cross containing fragments of a Saint's bone, then finally he comes in with the village priest bearing the Holy Sacrament. At the foot of the bed stands my mother staring at me with eyes full of misery. Twice she breaks down ringing her hands:

"I cannot bear to see my own child suffer so," she cries brokenly and is quickly led out of the room.

Our old professor is there too and my maid, and the nurse, and all the older servants who have known me since my birth. The nursery seems full of people. Baby is choking, there are no oxygen bags and I breathe into his mouth to help a little. Hands try to pull me back, voices say: "What are you doing, don't you know the contagion is deadly?"

But I push those hands away. "Contagion?" I cry desperately, "what does that mean, who cares? Don't you see my baby's choking? . . ."

Then minutes of respite, when suddenly the blue eyes open wide and stare back into mine, when a smile breaks the parched lips and makes them bleed, and a strange baby voice, in the voice of diphtheria, whispers: "Tell about Gingo" and "Sing a song of sixpence." And from some unknown, amazing source I draw the strength to "tell about Dingo," yellow dog Dingo, how he runs fast, always faster and grins like a coal skuttle. And I sing the song of sixpence until the smile fades away, the eyes close in pain, the deadly choking begins again and I have to breathe into his mouth to help him through his agony.

"Still ran Dingo, yellow dog Dingo, always faster, always running faster, grinning like a rat trap. . . ." "Sing a song of sixpence a pocket full of rye" . . . and "breathe, breathe, breathe" into that small gasping mouth, that is all I know, all I can do and all that I can think about during those last hours. Then suddenly the baby opens his eyes again, sits up in his crib, stretches out his arms. "Oh, pretty, pretty," he chuckles gleefully and falls back.

The hands that have been pulling at me from time to time now grasp me firmly. The voices say, in what seems an incredible chorus in a nightmare:

"It's all over, come, come away."

"All over, what is all over?" I ask impatiently. "I don't understand." Then suddenly I do. In despair I throw myself down on my knees, and the last thing I remember is the taste of shoe polish on my lips as I wildly kiss the doctor's shiny black boots. "Save, oh, save my baby!" I hear my voice crying. Then all is a blank. I am stricken with diphtheria too and mercifully unconscious for days.

Fiery visions of pain, they pass away and I find myself still staring into the starlit sky out of the window of the Sidewater Hotel.

One night at the Sidewater Hotel I was awakened by weird sounds coming from the room next to mine (where lived a highly respectable-looking, very elderly couple whom occasionally I met in the corridor), sounds of raucous laughter, singing, cursing, wrestling and even slapping. Yes, unmistakably I could hear heavy hand slaps on bare flesh, followed by shrieks of laughter and wild curses. Those unnatural sounds made me feel sick; terrified I listened and then unable to stand it any longer, dressed hurriedly and ran downstairs to the night manager.

"Come quick, something awful is happening in the room next to mine," I gasped, and obligingly he followed me upstairs accompanied by the house detective. There, all three, we stood silently outside my neighbor's door through which the sounds of uncanny laughter, songs, shrieks, slappings and crashing of china, glass and furniture came louder than ever.

"Oh, what *is* it?" I whispered in terror, but the manager merely shrugged his shoulders and smiled.

"It's all right, don't be afraid. The old folks are only

drunk and celebrating," he whispered back soothingly. "But I'll see that it never happens again . . . and perhaps you'd better move into another room for the rest of this night."

Gratefully I accepted the offer, and with his help and that of the house detective carried my things to a room further down the corridor. The next day I met the old couple in the elevator. They were looking, as usual, very grave and dignified, and it was hard to believe that only the previous night they had disported themselves so shamefully and had made so much unseemly noise.

"Slappers," I thought to myself as I watched them out of the tail of my eye. "Nasty old slappers, that's what you really are, you pompous old hypocrites." And from that day on they became "The Slappers" to me. And as long as I live I shall never forget the naughty song they sang that night.

My Real Estate venture did not last long. After several months of fruitless endeavors to sell those wretched lots I gave it up in despair and began to search for some other kind of work. At last after a month of frantic "looking around" for something appropriate to do I was offered the position of hostess in one of the most fashionable and exclusive dressmaking establishments in Metropole. Situated on the main thoroughfare, in a three-storied house all of its own, with tall glass windows in which were discreetly exhibited a few choice articles of apparel: a dress, for instance, on a painfully distorted gilt mannequin; an evening wrap thrown nonchalantly across a Louis XVI arm chair of unmistakably new make, a fan and a few trinkets, this "Maison de Couture" was supposed to be the acme of elegance where all the millionairesses young and old bought their clothes and hats. A doorman in uniform guarded the entrance and also ushered the distinguished guests up the short flight of stairs into the long show room. It was here, practically at the head of those steps and in the manner of a second glorified doorman that I, in my new rôle of hostess, was expected to meet the ladies and "with a pleasant smile and a few affable words" (according to the instructions given me) lead them gently towards their various salesladies. I had to know, and that was considered very important, which saleslady was the favorite of which customer, and woe betide me if I made a mistake. That was unpardonable in the eyes of both customer and saleslady, and my frequent errors would be met by glares and mutterings on either side. One woman (and how I would love to name her!) used to make it a special point of brushing me aside as I greeted her at the door with my professional "affable smile" and then—while, obedient to instructions, I accompanied her down the show room to the fitting rooms, trying to think of something pleasant to say—she would invariably mutter:

"Stop following me, I know where I'm going, you . . ." and I must confess that the last word, barely whispered, sounded to me always very much like "fool."

For a while my position was precarious, as the rôle of hostess was an innovation that displeased most of the old customers. Several women complained to the owner that they did not want to be met at the door like strangers,—that they knew perfectly well whom they wanted to see and what they wanted to buy when they entered the "Establishment" and that the hostess only bothered them. All of which created an awful situation for me. If I did *not* meet the fair ladies, then the manager Mr. Timson scolded me and threatened to fire me. If I *did* meet them, they would grumble and complain. At last I compromised on greeting them with a bow in the middle of the room and then walking behind them in silence. But that made me feel very uncomfortable for I realized that I was not earning my salary.

My fellow workers were numerous and of the most varied types. First came the manager, Mr. Harold Timson, a tall lanky Englishman whose queerly-knit figure seemed to be going to pieces in the most alarming fashion every time he moved. Mostly he spent his days sitting behind a desk in the small office back of the fitting rooms, looking very important and speaking in masterful tones into a dictaphone. As most of the French gowns of "Delphine's" were made in Omaha at a ridiculously low price and then relabeled "Paris" and sold at exorbitant prices to the gullible millionairesses of Metropole, Mr. Timson's letters were chiefly dictated for the benefit of the unfortunate Omaha workers who toiled so generously for the glory of France. Sometimes he would emerge from his office and then the uncanny trick he had of throwing out his long spindly legs 'way ahead of his body, would fascinate me to such an extent that I'd find myself watching anxiously for the next step he would make. His progress across the principal show room was a sight not easily forgotten, especially when he'd throw out one large flat foot a little too far ahead and catch it in a piece of furniture or, worse still, in the folds of an elaborate "Omaha-Paris" gown, innocently draped on one of the dress hangers. Then he would storm and wave his extraordinary-looking arms and accuse the frightened salesladies and impudent mannequins of "carelessly, purposely and maliciously" obstructing his dignified advance. Once in the midst of such a scene he caught sight of me choking with irreverent laughter and turned his wrath in my direction. His denunciating words should have "reduced me to ashes" but instead I only exploded with an unseemly burst of merriment and fled into the locker room. After that he did not speak to me for a very long while.

Miss Millicent Wintergreen, the owner of "Delphine's," a languid, exotic and prominent society leader of Metropole, used to arrive every morning about ten o'clock wrapped in marvelous furs, heavily scented with expensive perfume, with a smile on her face for the entire staff, who usually rushed forward to greet her as she came in. It was a beautiful, pained and patient smile which always made me wonder whether the "pain" part of it was caused by the general inefficiency of her employees of which I was the worst. After she had wafted past our obsequiously bowing group she would drift upstairs into her own, luxuriously comfortable private office and remain there all day long, unseen and unheard. Then about five o'clock she would descend in her inimitable drifting, wafting way and gently smile at us again with the same beautiful, pained and patient smile. The door man who, was known as Frederick to the customers and as Fred to the employees, would accompany her to her discreetly elegant limousine and then return to his post snapping his fingers, whistling gayly for the first time that day and usually remarking in a loud and disrespectful voice: "And that's that!"

It was he who always warned us of Miss Wintergreen's arrival in the morning by sticking his head through the door and shouting vociferously, "Hey, everybody, she's here!" Then he'd run to her car, help her out and respectfully assist her up the steps into the show room. Sometimes she did not come at all and then

Fred would have a grand time whistling softly all day between the arrival of customers, reading pink scandal sheets, munching peanuts or chewing gum. Somehow Mr. Timson's long legs never carried him as far as Fred's domain and therefore he was never reprimanded. All the salesladies, mannequins and work-girls liked Fred as much as I did for he was always nice and obliging and whenever he could, willingly ran errands for all of us. Many times he would open his door at the foot of the steps and in a loud whisper offer to bring me a sandwich or a bar of chocolate because he thought that I looked "sorta tired and peaked standin' there all day."

The salesladies were at first somewhat antagonistic and unfriendly towards me but soon that wore off and we got on well together. Mrs. Dickson, my favorite one, was a tall, dark-haired, rather handsome woman in her late forties. She was intelligent, always good-natured, very kindly, even-tempered, humorous and most entertaining. She took a liking to me, called me "Tish," comforted me when she saw that I was unhappy and, like Fred, offered me things to eat, or urged me to sit down when she noticed that my ankles were badly swollen from standing all day long.

The second saleslady, Mrs. Nilson, was of a different type in every way. Small, dainty, pretty, with fluffy gray hair,—very gray, although she too was only in her forties,—she was fond of chatter, gossip and spicy

stories. She was having a lot of trouble with her husband, an automobile salesman, and every morning
would regale us with fresh details of her marital woes.
She wore pretty clothes, was inordinately proud of her
small, well-shod feet, adored gayety and excitement
and always made me think of a little twittering, chirruping bird that constantly preened its brilliant feathers.

The third saleslady, Miss Brown, was like a mouse
with her bright beady eyes, soft brown hair, small sharp-
pointed teeth and general air of unassuming modesty,
sly reserve and furtive secrecy. She worked steadily,
silently with quiet rapid gestures, was polite to every
one, though not especially pleasant to any one in particular, and scampered away whenever she heard Mr.
Timson's voice raised in anger, quietly smiling to herself while others did the talking. A "Sainte n'y touche"
I thought she was until the evening I came on her un-
awares, in the dark little restaurant where I used to
eat my modest suppers, and found her holding affec-
tionately the hand of a large, fat, benevolent gentleman
unmistakably of the type commonly known as "Sugar
Daddy."

"Oh," she cried in dismay, as she saw me pass their
table and then ran up to me and begged me not to tell
any one, for, as she confided ecstatically in my ear, he
was her Sugar Daddy and no mistake about that!

The two salesladies in the hat department were elderly, efficient and motherly, while their assistant, a good-looking, dashing young woman soon left the great house of "Delphine" to marry a rich young man about town.

Upstairs, in the two very special show rooms next to Miss Wintergreen's office were two more salesladies, dignified and elderly who had been with Miss Wintergreen ever since the day that "Delphine" had opened its impressive doors to its no less impressive public. These ladies were very high and mighty, took care of only the "cream of the cream" of Metropole's society and paid us downstairs no attention whatsoever.

After the salesladies came the mannequins, all young and beautiful, of course, with lovely figures and perfect hands and feet. Maresa, who drew the highest salary and was therefore considered most important of all, was a tall, exceptionally slender girl with great flashing black eyes, raven black hair, small nose, tiny mouth, flawless teeth and the loveliest cream-colored complexion I have ever seen. I nicknamed her "the kitten," because of her supple, feline movements and her curious way of laughing softly down her throat, that sounded just exactly like the purring of a cat. It was amusing to see her next to Miss Brown and watch them talk to each other. I used to speculate whether in previous incarnations they had really been cat and mouse. But though Maresa's exterior was extremely beautiful and sophisticated, her speech was as simple and primitive as her mind, and from her cherry-like lips I learned a large vocabulary of amazing words ordinarily not used in polite society. She was so utterly sure of her supremacy over all the other mannequins that it never occurred to her child-like mind to be jealous or ruffled about anything they did. Any kind of dress looked perfect on her and it was amusing to see some fat old woman buy the dress Maresa was modeling because she thought she would look well in it too.

Then there was Hilda Stefenson, the Swedish girl, who possessed a face and figure so purely Grecian, so absolutely divine in the flawless beauty reminiscent of an Olympian goddess, that it was a breath-taking delight to watch her parade up and down the room in the white and silver draperies that she was wisely made to wear. She was a clever, well-educated girl and worked as a mannequin only because she wanted to earn enough money to be able to finish her last year in college. I used to talk a great deal with her and was immensely touched one day, when a year later, after we had both left "Delphine's," she wrote me a perfectly beautiful letter thanking me for having inspired her by my "noble example of patience and fortitude." It was nice to think that I *had* inspired some one in my rôle of super-doorman and her kind words were like balm on the painful memories of my Delphinian past. Interest-

[257]

ing too were the different types of customers, who passed me, as in a kaleidoscope, from morning until evening. Old ladies, filled with the sense of their own tremendous importance, some hugely fat, others painfully thin, usually wearing extraordinary-looking old-fashioned hats belonging to the days of their youth, hats with high crowns richly decorated with ribbons and plumes and which their owners always wore tilted downwards in the direction of their dignified noses. After a visit from one of those venerable customers the hat department would groan in chorus and complain bitterly that again a Victorian atrocity had been ordered, with instructions to make it as much like the old one as possible and that no amount of tactful persuasion had induced the old lady to permit "Delphine" to modernize her antiquated style of head gear. Then there would be the middle-aged women, mostly demanding something "youthful" and angrily repudiating hats that made them look "too old"; and the young women who carelessly bought any hat that was becoming. And it was the same way with the dresses. The old ladies who had been customers for years were always taken care of by the two high and mighty personages upstairs and as a result would order the same kind of gowns year after year, and the middle-aged women would select the most youthful-looking clothes, while the young married women and girls chose "anything that looked well."

Some were more polite and pleasant to the hard-working salesladies than others; a few were even quite nice and human, but as a rule nearly all were impatient, supercilious and very often capricious. I'll never forget the afternoon when Mrs. Nilson had to go home on account of a bad headache and I was asked to take her place and sell dresses. I soon found out that the customer most difficult to please was the one who had brought her friend along "to help choose a few rags." Usually the friend would be extremely critical and, sitting on a chair next to the tall mirror in the fitting room, would "pick to pieces" one dress after the other. Rapidly smoking cigarettes she'd speak in a perfectly audible undertone regardless of the saleswoman, in fact usually speaking *at* her like this:

"Simply hideous, my dear! *Tell her* that you are not accustomed to such dresses and that she's to bring in something decent. . . . *Tell her* you prefer red. . . . *Tell her* that if she has nothing better to show we'll go elsewhere. Why, you couldn't wear that rag to a dog fight! Some people have no ideas whatsoever, stupid, you know," and so on in that same vein with hardly a pause for breath. When I first heard that rude "tell her" I was so indignant that I ran to Mrs. Dickson nearly crying, but she only laughed and said:

[259]

"Never mind, Tish, that happens to all of us twenty times a day, if not oftener. Just pretend you don't hear, don't pay any attention, don't answer and don't let them see you're hurt."

And with this new philosophy based on a lot of "don'ts" I had to be content.

Some of the customers played little tricks on us all of their own and very nasty little tricks they were! For instance one very well-known, very rich woman chose an elaborate, expensive rhinestone diadem which she intended wearing to the opera that same night.

"Charge it, wrap it up and give it to me at once—I'll wear it this evening," she said imperatively to Mrs. Nilson who was "taking care" of her and accordingly Mrs. Nilson had the diadem wrapped up and handed it to Mrs. X. to take home with her. Early next morning before Miss Wintergreen's arrival as we were looking through the picture section of the newspaper, we all saw several photographs of Mrs. X. in the rhinestone diadem that she had purchased at "Delphine's." What was our surprise an hour later, when the lady in question appeared carrying the diadem, which according to the newspapers she had worn the previous night at the opera, and which now she calmly handed to Mrs. Nilson saying:

"I couldn't think of wearing a cheap thing like that after all. When I tried it on in front of my own mirror at home last night I saw it was all wrong, so I brought it back. Strike it off my bill, don't forget to do that."

Aghast I looked at Mrs. Dickson but she only shrugged her shoulders and later on remarked:

"And *that* kind of thing happens very often too."

One day Mr. Timson had the horrible idea of making me look up all the addresses and telephone numbers of our customers in the telephone directory and then check them up with the cards on file, a wretched job that took me days and days to accomplish. As he had plenty of office girls for that kind of work, he probably made me do it to revenge himself for the time when I laughed at him in front of everybody else, and a worse revenge he could not have invented. After hours of poring over that endless book, I'd get so fidgety I could hardly sit still, while names and numbers danced in front of my tired eyes. At last Mrs. Dickson, unable to stand it any longer, told Miss Wintergreen about it and she sent word that I should stop immediately, as looking up addresses had absolutely nothing to do with my duties of hostess. And as a climax Marie, the little stock girl, came running up to me and whispered in my ear with glee that Mr. Timson had been severely reprimanded by Miss Wintergreen for making me do something that I was not supposed to do. Funny little Marie, with her face like a cameo, her mottled complexion, her short sturdy figure and her habit of

[261]

constantly singing softly under her breath the same song over and over again:

"Maybe he'll phone me,
Maybe he'll call me,
Maybe he'll radio-o-o"

Often I used to wonder whether "he" ever did "phone, call or radio," and hoped he was good to her for she was such a nice little girl.

After a few idiotic months of being hostess, that is, a doorman of less consequence than Fred, who after all *did* open and close doors, assist ladies to their cars and help them up the steps, I was offered the position of assistant to an interior decorator, which I joyfully accepted. I was sorry to say good-by to the salesladies and mannequins of whom I had grown fond, but it was a relief to think that my "affable smiles and pleasant speeches" were really at an end and that at last I could look forward to some genuine, sensible work.

My new employer, Mrs. Burton, was an energetic little woman of about fifty, with gray hair, pink cheeks and a pince-nez that constantly slipped down her nose. She was nervous and high strung, but nearly always cheerful and a very hard worker. Her small apartment, in one of the new houses, situated only a few blocks away from the fashionable section where lived the millionaires, consisted of a diminutive entrance hall, a narrow drawing room, a larger room that served both as bedroom and dining room, and a little office, sandwiched in between the bathroom and kitchen. It was in this office that I was to sit all day, answering the telephone, laboriously typing letters with one finger and keeping the files in order. As Mrs. Burton was of good family and well connected she worked almost entirely for very wealthy people and, during my stay with her, decorated quite a few elaborate apartments and even houses. After telling me what to do early in the morning, she would usually disappear until five o'clock, tearing all over town in her old Ford "Lizzie," scampering hither and yon in a frenzy of activity, doing a hundred things in one hour, never resting, never relaxing, but always "on the go," as busy as a squirrel. Sometimes she would return at noon and give me new directions, or else carry me off to lunch with her, but that was not often, and mostly I'd spend my days all alone in the tiny office. Except when the telephone rang I wouldn't hear a sound for hours, and as I did not have much work to do (neither did I consider that I could read or write during working hours), time dragged fearfully and I'd become very restless and watch the clock with impatience. Once a strange thing happened, something that makes me feel badly to this day. It was like this:

I was sitting at my desk typing one of those interminable letters that interior decorators write to the houses that supply them with goods (Johnson and Faulkner, Cheney's etc.) when all of a sudden the telephone rang and a man's voice asked for Mrs. Burton. When I told him that she was out he seemed to be very much amused at my Russian accent and after telling me so, kept me talking for quite a while. After that he used to call me up every afternoon and as I was terrifically bored sitting all day long in that stuffy little office, his amusing conversation was quite a welcome interruption, and I finally began to look forward to it. Mrs. Burton had told me that he was "perfectly all right," middle-aged, a gentleman, in fact a friend of hers, so that I saw no reason to discourage his daily talks, especially as he never made any attempt to see me. Once he complained that he had caught a bad cold and when I recommended aspirin he laughed a lot, because he said that my way of pronouncing it "aspireen" and of rolling the r in it was "just too funny for words." "Say aspirin," he pleaded over and over again until I grew annoyed and hung up the receiver. These daily conversations must have lasted about three or four months. At last one morning he asked me whether I'd have lunch with him the following week and named a certain day. As I had grown to like him and was curious to see what he looked like, I accepted his invitation and was much amused at his very juvenile shouts of delight down the telephone. However when that day arrived, Mrs. Burton, who was sick in bed, asked me to do an important errand for her and as it had to be done immediately I called up Mr. X. and not finding him at home left word with his servant that I would not be able to meet him, according to our agreement, outside my office. It had never entered my mind that he would make any special preparations for that lunch; in fact, I thought that we would probably go to my usual haunt, the little sandwich shop around the corner.

What was my horror when on returning from the errand about three o'clock Mr. X. called me up and in a perfectly heartbroken voice said that I had spoiled the one great pleasure he had been looking forward to with such delight.

"I had planned to bring you to my own house," he positively sobbed. "There were roses on the table, my best china, glass, silver and champagne, caviar . . . oh, how could you be so cruel! What have you done? You'll never know what you have done to me."

Surprised, dismayed, I apologized as best I could, though on the other hand I felt slightly angered at the thought that he had planned such an elaborate reception without letting me know anything about it. At last with the unmanly words:

"I'm crying! I wish you could see me, the tears are streaming down my face, good-by," shouted into my

[265]

astounded ear, he hung up the receiver, and, very crest-fallen and somewhat annoyed, I soon went home.

It all seemed such a fuss about nothing. What if I *had* been unable to come that day to lunch, surely there were other days!

"He is positively childish, ridiculous," I thought and tried to dismiss the episode from my mind.

However, next day I was surprised not to hear from him as usual, then a second day passed, a third, a fourth, a week, two weeks! Finally I called up his number.

"May I speak to Mr. X?" I asked when an un-familiar voice answered the telephone.

"Mr. X.?" it said slowly as though surprised at my question. "Mr. X., why, he's ill, dying—didn't you know that?"

Puzzled, I asked Mrs. Burton that evening whether she knew that Mr. X. was so seriously ill.

"Why, yes," she replied. "It all started about two weeks ago, most mysteriously. He said then that he had had a bitter disappointment and began drinking. He drank steadily for ten days, then something dreadful happened: an ulcer in his stomach opened, he had peritonitis and now he is dying. I'm glad you reminded me, I'll call up and find out how he is."

She took up the receiver and asked for his number while I listened anxiously.

"How is Mr. X. to-night?" I heard her inquire, then:

"Oh, no! Not really? When? Oh, dear, oh, dear!"

"Is he dead?" I asked shakily.

"Yes," she answered, and then began to cry.

While she was crying I tiptoed out of the room, and as it was nearly six o'clock left for home. All that night I couldn't sleep. I seemed to hear his voice laughing, teasing, pleading, telling funny stories "to cheer you up in your loneliness, Cinderella," he would say. Then to my surprise I started to cry too and cried over the death of a man whom I had never seen in all my life and would never, never see alive. I could not go to his funeral for Mrs. Burton went, and there was no excuse for me to leave the office, but a few days later, on a Saturday afternoon, I bought some roses, thinking ruefully about the roses that he had bought to decorate his lunch table, and carried them to his grave. A man was sitting there, an oldish man with red eyes, dressed in a shabby overcoat, who stared at me curiously as I came up and placed my sheaf of roses on the freshly made mound. Then after a few minutes' silence he suddenly spoke:

"Are you the lady who was to have had lunch with *him* two weeks ago?" he inquired dully, in a curiously impersonal, dead sort of voice, pointing at the grave as he said "him"—and as I nodded he continued in the same toneless way: "Well, then you should know that *that* finished him, the disappointment I mean. He never got over it. Why, he was so happy, so excited about your coming, just like a boy. . . . Made me change that table a dozen times. . . . 'James,' he'd say, 'I think it looks better this way,' and then I'd have to do it all over again. Roses, yes, sir, two dozen American Beauties . . . and champagne and everything that was best. He even had me get his silver table centerpiece from the bank. I had to bring it home in a taxi it was so heavy. And all for nothing! You wouldn't come. . . ."

"Not 'wouldn't come' but couldn't come," I corrected him softly.

And so we stood side by side—the faithful servant of a man whom I had never known and I, who had been the indirect, unconscious cause of the inexplicable sorrow that had brought him to an untimely end.

Several other strange things happened to me that winter. As by that time I knew a great many people in Metropole and was free to do as I pleased in the evenings, I went out a good deal although I never stayed late.

It was then that I formed many pleasant friendships which happily counterbalanced the decidedly *un*pleasant episodes that were quite plentiful that year. The first one that seemed to start the ghastly series (following the sad story of Mr. X.'s demise) began at a dinner party, where unfortunately I attracted the attention of a certain Mr. Reeves Tray, popular widower and a minor sardine king. Tall and exceptionally ugly, with small blue eyes and an enormous red nose, he sat by my side all evening long, gazing at me approvingly and whispering what he himself termed "sweet nothings."

Shortly after that first encounter he began to write me little notes and frequently sent me flowers. At last one morning I received from him a formal invitation to dinner, which I happened to show to two very kindly old ladies who had taken a great liking to me.

"Oh, by all means accept," they both cried in one breath. "He gives the loveliest dinner parties that are always the talk of the town. Some charming woman will preside as hostess; there will be music. Last year he had some wonderful Italian guitar players, and altogether you will have a delightful time."

So I accepted.

As the dinner was to be at a small, exclusive club, somewhat out of the way of my regular mode of transportation—the bus, I decided to "splurge" recklessly for once and hired a taxi. Arriving at the club at exactly half-past seven I was surprised not to see a long line of cars drawing up to the main entrance,—in fact, but for my taxi with its bright headlights, the street was dark and quite deserted. Thinking that perhaps I had been mistaken about the date of the dinner party I hastily consulted the invitation that I had in my evening bag.

But no, I was not mistaken, both date and address were correct, so I got out of the taxi, and not without misgivings, entered the club. At the door a fat old man-servant greeted me and smiling benevolently, in fatherly tones directed me to the ladies' room where I was to deposit my wrap. Then that having been accomplished with the help of a discreet-looking maid, another servant took charge of me and led me across a long dimly lighted ball room into a diminutive dining room that reminded me most unpleasantly of a *cabinet particulier*. Here I found my sardine king, in solitary grandeur, dressed in his best bib and tucker with a white gardenia in the lapel of his swallow-tail coat and beaming delightedly as he advanced to meet me with outstretched hands. Behind him stood a small table conspicuously laid for two.

"Welcome, my dear little countess, welcome!" he cried effusively, kissing my hand, or rather wiping his big red nose on it. Then, dinner being announced, he led me ceremoniously up to an imposing-looking gilt arm-chair in which I, somewhat gingerly, sat down. Followed what my host called "a cozy little dinner," but which in reality turned out to be a long and complicated meal with wine and champagne and delicacies out of season. As one rich course followed the other I involuntarily thought of my thirty-cent lunches in the sandwich shop "around the corner" and of the modest breakfasts and suppers that I myself now cooked on the small electric heater in my room.

"What are you thinking of, fair countess?" asked my host, bending towards me confidentially with a rather alarming gleam in his "piggy" eyes.

"I'm thinking of a nice little place where I can get lunch for thirty cents," I answered gravely, and was pleased to see that he appeared somewhat disconcerted at such an unpoetic reply. Again and again he tried to introduce a topic of conversation worthy of his dinner, and of the discreetly intimate surroundings in which he had so hopefully placed me, but again and again my flat, prosaic replies struck the wrong note and frustrated all his noble efforts. At last, as the dinner was drawing to an end he gloomily asked me whether I'd rather "sit here and talk," or else "go to the theater and see Mr. Gallagher and Mr. Shean in person."

"Oh, the theater of course," I cried with such alacrity that he stared at me in pained surprise and then loudly, even rudely I thought, ordered his car to be brought around at once.

But as we were driving down a dimly lighted street he dashingly played his last card in the pretty little *jeu gallant* that he had so carefully planned and taking my hand into his own large, soft and moist one, gave it a most unpleasant squeeze.

"Oh, please don't, it hurts, and your hand is so hot

[271]

and damp!" I cried, pulling mine out with great energy. And that finished it all—once and forever. Drawing himself up with dignity into the far away corner of the car, he lapsed into a stony silence that lasted until the end of the evening. While I watched gleefully the antics of Mr. Gallagher and Mr. Shean and thoroughly enjoyed myself, he sat straight up in his seat, mutely indignant, sternly disapproving and with the expression "I am deeply offended" plainly written all over his face. Only once did he open his lips, and that was to bid me good-by as he placed me in a taxi homeward bound.

A few weeks later, however, wishing to repay him for his lavish entertainment, I wrote to him asking him to dine with me and the man whom I was soon going to marry. His reply, stating regrets, was couched in the briefest and stiffest words, which were the last I ever received from him.

Only much later did I discover that my cronies, the two elderly ladies, had been desperately busy matchmaking and had tried their best to bring the sardine king to "propose to me honorably" and offer me his generous hand and heart. But as the old ladies somewhat shamefacedly confessed to me a year later, he never viewed the situation from that angle, his intentions from beginning to end having been "strictly dishonorable."

BETROTHAL PICTURE OF MY MOTHER AND FATHER

After that came the sad episode with a gentleman ranking high in the slaughter-house business, with whom my first meeting was one afternoon when he presented himself in my little office and mournfully announced that he had "bad news" for me and would I please sit down. Frightened, with shaking knees and my voice gone, I motioned him to proceed, while I sank into Mrs. Burton's arm-chair, wondering wildly which member of my own family had suddenly passed away. After several false starts and a few maddening "hems and haws" that nearly drove me frantic, he finally delivered himself of his amazing news which turned out to be nothing more than a rumor that he had heard, a rumor (which later proved to be untrue) that my ex-husband's second wife had died of appendicitis.

"And is that all?" I fairly shrieked, jumping out of the arm-chair and wishing with all my heart that I could wring his neck, for though I had no ill feelings whatsoever towards my ex-husband's (Count Keller's) second wife, still I was hardly enough interested in her to be glad to be subjected to such a fearful scare.

"Why, yes!" answered the gentleman, somewhat surprised at the way I was taking his news, "that's all. I hope I did not shock you?"

"You certainly did," I replied quite sharply, for by this time my fright had turned to annoyance, and I was really provoked at the man for having upset me so badly, for nothing. "You did! I thought something dreadful had happened. But why on earth did you suppose that I would be particularly interested in the fate of my ex-husband's present wife?" I continued, feeling more and more aggrieved as he gazed at me with a bland smile and murmured:

"Oh, all right, don't get peeved, I just thought you'd like to know, that's all. And by the way, my name is Gilbertson Fillet and I know many Russians abroad, in London and Paris and Vienna,—for I travel a good deal and make a special point of meeting your people. Nicest people in the world, I think."

"Is that why you called on me?" I demanded, beginning to see the light and not at all surprised when he calmly answered "yes" and promptly invited me to lunch. I nearly burst out laughing—it was so absurd! First poor Mr. X., then the Sardine man and now this one, all starting the same way, by offering me some food.

"They certainly must think that the way to a penniless Russian's heart is through her stomach," I thought pensively, gazing at my rotund, ruddy-cheeked, white-haired new acquaintance, and wondering if he too would ply me with delicacies out of season and rare wines.

"Just a simple little lunch at the club," I heard him suggest persuasively, but I firmly refused the invitation, saying that I had too much work to do. And though he departed then with many apologies for having disturbed me, that was by no means the end of our acquaintance. Flowers and candy and the inevitable little notes began to trickle in, and nearly everywhere I went in the evening I'd meet him, resplendent with unusually large diamonds or rubies or emeralds blazing away in his stiff shirt front. I did not really dislike him, though he was rather blatant in many ways: for instance he once put me into a taxi and handed me a ten-dollar bill saying: "Pay the driver and keep the change," and another time he shouted publicly and very rudely at the head waiter in a restaurant for not bringing him immediately what he had asked for, roaring to the top of his voice that he was Gilbertson Fillet himself (though he was only a guest and not the host of the party), and then insisted on showing every one, with many knowing winks, the photograph of a well-known society woman, that he carried in his breast pocket. But on the other hand I knew that he had been very kind to several of my unfortunate compatriots and tried to persuade myself that it was not his fault that he had such regrettable manners. However it all ended as far as I was concerned, after a dinner to which he too, like the Sardine King, had invited me most formally.

"Who's coming?" I asked suspiciously over the telephone when I read his invitation and was relieved to hear the names of two very dignified couples.

The dinner was supposed to be held in the main

dining room of the fashionable hotel in which he was staying, for, as he traveled a great deal he did not live in a house or an apartment, but preferred having rooms at a hotel. As I came into the lobby I was met by his secretary, who, bowing politely asked me to step into the elevator as: "Cocktails before dinner were being served in Mr. Fillet's own drawing room," he said. On the threshold of his employer's suite the secretary bowed again and left me standing face to face with my host, alone.

"Why, where are all your other guests? Am I too early?" I asked abruptly, wondering if I had again walked stupidly into another gallant trap.

"Oh, dear countess, I'm dreadfully sorry, but at the last minute they found out they could not come," answered Mr. Fillet sadly. "But I thought that you and I could have a pleasant little dinner together, so I canceled the table downstairs and ordered dinner to be sent up here. You don't mind, do you?" he continued, taking me up to a small table that looked ridiculously like the one Mr. Reeves Tray had arranged, as even the floral decorations were exactly the same.

"Idiot," I said, admonishing myself angrily. "Idiot, how can you be such an infernal fool as to get yourself into such a situation twice running, just like a silly girl, and you in your 'sophisticated' thirties!" I went on jeering silently at my own stupidity.

As long as the dinner lasted everything was all right, for Mr. Fillet loved to eat and paid more attention to his food than to any guest he might be entertaining, but when that meal was over he became quite horrid.

First he wanted me to lie down on his sofa because, according to him, I looked tired, then when I flatly refused to do that, he suddenly went into the bedroom, threw himself on his bed and started to moan in a most alarming fashion.

"What is the matter?" I called from the drawing-room, but he only moaned the louder, gasping:

"Oh, I feel so ill, so ill."

At last, horrified at the thought that perhaps he was really dying there and that I would be the last person to see him alive—I went into his room and bent over him suspiciously.

"What on earth has happened to you? Is it indigestion?" I demanded. "I'm a medical person and if you don't stop groaning immediately I'll send for your secretary and the manager and a doctor," I said as forcibly as I could. And that worked like a charm. Springing off his bed, in the pink of health as I had suspected, he glared at me furiously.

"You little devil," he cried, "you know perfectly well what is the matter with me and you stand there calmly making fun of me. You look feminine enough, but goodness knows there's nothing feminine about you!

I was crazy with a wild desire to kiss you, but now I would as soon kiss my valet." Whereupon having satisfied myself that Mr. Gilbertson Fillet was not expiring I grabbed my hat and gloves and joyfully fled.

After that there were two more unpleasant incidents of that same order. First when the eminent lawyer and politician Mr. Hornblower Trump (into whose office I had come by appointment to get my papers prolonging my stay in the United States) locked his door, put out his spidery arms and in a maudlin voice asked me whether I'd like to be the inspiration of a great man, whose wife did not understand him. But I pushed the great man in his flowery waistcoat, ran to the door, unlocked it and once more fled from the presence of another silly old man. A few days later, however, I met him in the house of mutual friends, where after managing to get me into a corner alone, he hissed angrily that he'd have me deported, as he had the power to do so.

"Oh, no, you won't," I retorted, "not after the way you have behaved. Don't you suppose that I'd tell all about that if you tried to harm me?" And with these words I triumphantly parted with the great Hornblower Trump forever.

The final episode of that kind occurred when a highly respectable old man about seventy calmly informed me at a dinner party (in fact his mouth was full at the time he said it) that he had conferred on me the honor of electing me his "dame de cœur." In amazement I stared at him and then actually did burst out laughing.

"Of course you would!" I cried. "I'm still young, healthy, not the ugliest person in the world, of good family, penniless, and with no one in my background to beat you up. An ideal combination for the delightful rôle you have offered me!" And somewhat taken aback at my frank outburst, which he evidently was afraid others would hear, he patted my hand soothingly and said it was all right with him if I didn't want to accept his proposal.

After all those horrid experiences I began to think more seriously than ever of marrying my nice Navy man. He was so unlike all the other men I had seen. Regularly, every six weeks, he would come all the way from the East to see me and talk over the probability of our marriage. But just because I was very fond of him I could not make up my mind. It did not seem right that he should marry me, when I had been married before and had passed through such unspeakable tragedies. Besides I was a few years older than he . . . No, we could not marry!

"It would not be fair to you; you should marry a beautiful American girl five years younger than you are," I would argue and then see him off at his train, crying myself sick as he left me standing alone on the platform.

[279]

At the end of that winter I lost my job again, for poor Mrs. Burton, who was more artistic than business-like, got into financial difficulties and could not any longer afford to pay me my salary. It was then that I applied for work in a large department store, one of the largest in America.

Though I had letters of introduction to the head of the store's Employment Bureau, I had to wait for a long while outside his office, as on the day I presented myself he happened to be in conference. So I sat patiently on a chair opposite his door in the narrow drafty passage, watching all the other applicants file past me as they entered the smaller offices, situated to the right and to the left of the main office where ruled the man whom I was to see. One after the other my fellow applicants would emerge again, some flushed with pleased expressions on their faces, while others came out looking pale and downcast. Success or failure was written on their countenances as clearly as in a silent movie and time passed quickly as I sat and watched them. After two hours, that seemed like twenty minutes thanks to my own private movie show, the conference broke up and I was admitted to the presence of the head of the Employment Bureau, Mr. Freeman, a tall lean man with an extremely thin, intelligent, pleasing face, who met me at the door and, politely offering me a chair, apologized for having kept me waiting such a length of time. Then he read my letters of introduction very attentively and after a few minutes of thoughtful silence, during which I could see that he was looking me over and sizing me up very carefully, he asked me where I would rather work.

"The art department would be the best for you," he went on pleasantly, "but unfortunately we have no vacancies there at present. Perhaps later on. . . . Now let me see: jewelry, antiques, pictures, china . . . no—no vacancies there either. The only thing I can suggest right now is that you work either in the dress department or in the fur department. Which would you prefer?" Whereupon remembering the dress vicissitudes of my poor salesladies at "Delphine's," I promptly answered:

"The fur department, please." And so the die was cast!

During the next few minutes Mr. Freeman busily wrote, telephoned and showed me how to fill in and where to sign certain papers that were to make me an official member of the great store. Then he summoned the head of the fur department, Mr. Makepeace, a good-looking man about forty with an abrupt and rather stern manner who, after a short conversation with Mr. Freeman, told me briefly that I could report the following morning at eight o'clock.

As my first impressions had been good and both men

had pleased me, I departed well satisfied with the way I had been introduced to my new work house—Metropole's biggest department store.

The following morning I got up half an hour earlier, breakfasted in a hurry and feeling quite excited at the prospect of my new venture, climbed on top of the bus that would, from now on, take me down town to the busy corner where stood my imposing-looking store. The long drive in the fresh air of early morning made me feel unusually good and it was with color in my sallow cheeks and a feeling of exhilaration that I got off the bus and joined the thick, steady stream of workers that was pouring into the store. After being hopelessly pushed and jostled and made to run in the wrong direction I finally reached the locker room where I was given a kind of narrow long cage with shelves in which to keep my hat and coat and any other possessions that I happened to bring along. Then I went up to the sixth floor, where an obliging youth showed me the way to the fur department. Here I presented myself to Mr. Makepeace, who promptly took me upstairs to the school, where in the course of three days I was expected to learn all the rules of the store, how to make out sales checks and how to handle customers.

"Spell chinchilla," I was asked that afternoon and: "If a yard of rabbit costs $1.15 how much will eight yards cost?" or: "How would you soothe an angry customer who considers himself insulted? . . ."

Satisfied that I could read and write and count properly and also cope with the various temperaments of the customers, I was allowed to graduate *magna cum laude* that same evening, an unusual honor which, as I was gravely told, the school conferred on only a very few. And so, equipped with a certain amount of store knowledge that I had acquired during that one, amazing day, I returned on the following morning to the fur department and modestly announced to Mr. Makepeace that I was ready to work. Dressed in a black jersey dress (only black and dark blue dresses were allowed during working hours) with white linen collar and cuffs and my hair brushed back as primly as possible, I was taken all around the fur department and presented to my new colleagues. There were a great many of them.

First came Mrs. Allright, the oldest member of the entire fur force, a white-haired brisk little old lady, who spoke in sharp, crisp tones, and moved around with greater rapidity than any of the younger women.

And there was Mrs. Haveabill, also quite elderly, but tall and stately and as silent as Mrs. Allright was loquacious. Both were looked upon as the star performers of the fur department and, like the two exclusive salesladies at "Delphine's," handled only customers of high standing and great wealth.

Then came the group of middle-aged ladies: Mrs. Humphy, short, taciturn and hard-working; and Mrs. Fellow, stout and handsome with gray hair elaborately piled on top of her head, always well-dressed, always conversational and often quite caustic and entertaining; and Miss Boy, kind and warm-hearted and ever so responsive to other people's troubles; and Mrs. Slipmore, brown-haired, brown-eyed, preoccupied and absent-minded; and two or three others who were not permanent members of the fur force but were constantly shifted around to other departments, when extra help was needed.

The third group of younger women was headed by Miss Foodman, the assistant buyer, a rather pretty girl of about twenty-eight, though her good looks were usually marred by an expression of unfriendliness and discontent. They were a bevy of attractive girls, most of them with a college education who, for some reason (probably because they knew their arithmetic well), were grouped together behind a large glass counter and sold furs by the yard.

Finally there was Marcia, the mannequin, tall and beautiful, but with a hard expression in her eyes and around her mouth that spoiled her beauty.

The men of the fur force were numerous too. After Mr. Makepeace came his assistant, Mr. Canon, who looked somewhat like a "sugar daddy," though whether he was one or not I don't know, never having exchanged ten words with him; and there was Mr. Mount, a delightful, white-haired, frail old gentleman with charming, kindly manners; and Mr. Loubé, the Frenchman, whose thin, sensitive, careworn face, like a fine etching in its frame of wavy iron-gray hair, always made me think of some medieval knight—*sans peur et sans reproche*. He had the manners of one too, for he was courtly and gallant unto the smallest details of his unromantic work. In some mysterious fashion he managed to carry an ungainly fur coat across the room with such natural grace that it was a pleasure to watch him, and often I admired his patience and politeness with customers of the worst type. I liked to talk to him too, and frequently followed his advice, for he was a true gentleman, an idealist, and understood life with the uncanny cleverness of his race. A Chevalier of the Legion of Honor, he came of good family and had known better days before the war had deprived him of nearly all his worldly goods. It was then that for the sake of his wife and children, whom he adored, he had migrated to America and landed as star salesman in the famous fur department of Metropole's gigantic store.

Then there was Mr. Coffee, a fatherly, benevolent, old soul; and Mr. Enery, young, slightly built, dark-haired, swarthy and always impertinent-looking; and a number of stock boys among which only two stand out in my memory: John, the serious-minded youth, who thought of nothing but his work and knew every single coat and every inch of fur "by the yard" in the whole department; and Billy, the Moody Bible student who *never* thought about his work, but moved as in a trance, dreaming of a glorious hereafter where there would be no stores, no fur coats, nothing of that kind, only wings and harps and hymns. He loved to preach too, and often we would find him standing behind a long row of fur coats in one of the closets, waving his arms wildly as he addressed an imaginary audience.

My work in the fur department was very different from any other kind of work that I had ever done. I was expected to show and sell fur coats and that was all I did from the time the store opened until half-past five when it closed. Even so, we usually had to stay on a little longer in order to wind up the day's work and I rarely got on to my bus before six o'clock. Then it took me nearly an hour to reach the Sidewater Hotel, and by the time I arrived there I would be so exhausted that after a quick supper, which I could hardly swallow, I'd crawl into bed and stretch out my swollen, aching legs. Oh, how my legs did ache those days! It was hard enough standing all day long at "Delphine's," but in the fur department I had to carry dozens of heavy coats besides, and their weight would invariably hurt my back and make my knees bend like those of an old work horse dragging too great a load. In the morning, after a good night's rest, I'd feel all right again and would look forward with pleasure to the long ride on top of the bus. Whether it was fine weather or bad, I always rode down that way and filled my lungs with a provision of fresh air that was to last me until evening when once more I'd climb on top of the bus, gasping like a half-dead fish, eager for a new supply of oxygen. In those days life for me was made up more of sensations than of any thoughts. It was pleasant to awaken in my pretty little room, with its creamy walls and pale green furniture covered with a gay flowery chintz, and watch through the wide window opposite my bed, "the dawn come up like thunder out of 'mist' across the bay." And it was pleasant to run barefoot over the soft velvet carpet that stretched the entire length of the floor, and indulge in the luxury of a shower bath, and then, after donning my black jersey work dress with its white linen collar and cuffs, have breakfast and get ready for the drive. And it was pleasant to sit on the roof of the bus in the front seat and for nearly a whole hour, revel in the buffeting of the wind. All that part of the morning was undoubtedly pleasant. But after eight o'clock my feelings would gradually undergo a change. The rush into the store, the jostling of the workers, the bustle in the locker room, the punching of the clock, the ride in the elevator to the sixth floor, where in tall glass cases the same little stuffed white polar bears would be the first to greet me in the strange mixed light of a department store early in the morning—a light half natural and half electric that hurt the eyes and made them smart,—the frantic scurrying of the stock boys up and down the floor, uncovering the coats, shaking them out and hanging them up in places where later on they would attract the eyes of the customers,—all these first impressions were like the mingling of various small themes in a prelude that would eventually unite in one mighty theme, that of the steady beating of a pulse in a monster called Drudgery. I could hear its muffled throb, reminding me of the African tom-tom of the desert, and as I stumbled along beneath the heavy coats I would mechanically fall into step again to the rhythm of that never-ceasing, merciless sound.

"Don't you hear it, Monsieur Loubé? Don't you hear that awful 'boom-boom, boom, boom'?" I would desperately ask the Frenchman. And he would gravely answer, "Yes." Then with a quick change of mood, shrugging his shoulders and laughing, he would advise me not to notice it.

"Don't listen to it; listen to the other sounds: the funny ones that are all around us too," he'd cry and draw my attention to something absurd that would make me laugh.

EDGEWOOD COTTAGE, MY AMERICAN HOME IN ST. DAVID'S, PA.

Coats from morning till night, nothing but coats to think about!

Soon I grew to know them all. In some of the huge closets were the cheaper ones: muskrats, racoons, Hudson seals, and those funny-looking things called "Korovà" (which in Russian means plain cow, only the accent is on the second syllable); and in other closets were the higher priced ones, that to me represented the great middle class in the world of coats: squirrels, lambs, seals, leopards, beavers; and finally, in a special room all by themselves, guarded by a heavy iron door near which constantly lurked our own private Sherlock Holmes, Johnnie the detective, lived the aristocrats: the minks, the ermines and the famous Russian sables. These were usually shown by Mrs. Allright and Mrs. Haveabill, for only their clients could afford to buy such expensive furs, but two or three times even I got in there, though each time ended in bitter disappointment. The worst one of all was when a much-bejeweled woman demanded to see the very best sable wrap we had, and, after keeping me in an agony of suspense as she carefully examined it, ended by purchasing three yards of rabbit fur to trim a dress.

Then there was the woman who made me show her dozens and dozens of coats until I thought at last my knees would give way under the strain. The fur department was an immense place and I must have covered miles that day as I hurried backwards and forwards to the different closets, hauling out all the coats that I could lay hands on and then bringing them to my customer while she sat in a comfortable arm-chair. Even the stock boys got tired of carrying away the pile of coats that she had turned down and that steadily accumulated on chairs around us, and grumbled at me for not making her buy something at last. I must have been at my ninety-ninth coat and was conscientiously extolling its merits in an exhausted voice that didn't sound to me much like my own, when all of a sudden I heard a muffled sob behind me and turning around saw my friend Lyta Barr sitting on a chair half hidden between two mountains of coats and actually crying.

"Why, Lyta," I called out anxiously, "what is the matter?"

But she only waved her hand whispering:

"Never mind me; I've lots of time, I'll wait, go on with your d—— work." And I was obliged to obey her.

At last the customer departed, not having bought one inch of fur, though she had taken up hours of my time and had looked at more coats than I usually showed in a week. The minute she left Lyta threw her arms around me, crying:

"Oh, you poor darling! I can't stand this, I simply can't! It's awful. Do you know that for more than an hour I have watched you drag those wretched things from every closet in the store and the sight has made me sick. If only you could see yourself now: your shoulders are bent, your legs are swollen and your face looks positively haggard and old. Oh, you shouldn't be slaving like that for such a woman, it is she who should be waiting on you!"

Whereupon picturing vividly the sad spectacle I presented, I began to feel so sorry for myself that I sat down next to Lyta, behind the last mountain of musk-rats that had not yet been cleared away, and also burst into tears.

But my work was not always as hard as that. Sometimes, on the contrary, a whole day would pass without having to show one single coat, and then I'd feel no better, as the mortification of turning in my sales-book at night with the words "no sales" written at the bottom of the page, would be quite as distressing as the fatigue of a hard day's work.

Lunch time was always a welcome hour that helped cut the day into two definite parts. After washing my hands and brushing my hair in the small lavatory on the sixth floor marked: "For employees only," I'd run up to the cafeteria situated on the top floor of the building, where we, the workers of the store, could get a fairly decent lunch for very little money. But the babel of voices and the clatter of dishes made such a terrific noise that we had to shout at the top of our voices in order to make ourselves heard, and the way we had to run around collecting trays, paper napkins, cutlery, plates and food, was so bewildering to me that I never got what I really wanted, but wildly grabbed the first thing in sight. A fruit salad, coffee and rolls was what I usually aimed for, but when a plate of baked beans, a glass of a milk and a piece of pie (all things that I heartily detested), would mysteriously find their way onto my tray, I wasn't ever surprised.

"Move on, move on!" the person behind me would yell as I'd pause to consider what I would rather have and then I'd get so flustered that besides reaching out for what I didn't want I would let things slide off my tray and scatter all over the floor.

Once in a while I went out to lunch in some little restaurant or sandwich shop in the vicinity of the store, but those places were usually so crowded that they were hardly any better than the cafeteria.

Curious things happened to me that winter too: a well-known actress suggested that I go on the stage; a very wealthy, elderly woman, whom I had only met once, came to the fur department and offered to supply me with her discarded clothes which she said she had worn only once or twice, a kind gesture that I refused, saying that I preferred wearing something that I had earned myself no matter how modest it was; a rather nice man about forty, who happened to be a scion of one of Metropole's most prominent gilt-edged families, having bought a fur coat from me, suddenly started calling on me most embarrassingly during my working hours and sent gardenias every day, which the stock boys delivered with knowing winks and wide grins. After a month of such chivalrous behavior the scion gravely proposed to me behind a Kangaroo coat and, when I politely declined the honor, painstakingly pointed out the advantages that a union with him would bring to me in my poverty-stricken condition. But his eloquence failed to convince me.

Then there was the excitement of chasing a shoplifter who had, not too cautiously, pocketed a few yards of some cheap fur and who, on being cornered by me turned out to be so shabby and sad-looking that after taking the fur away from him I weakly let him go.

And there was the insolent man with fat red cheeks and a curly black mustache who after donning a brand new raccoon coat for which he had not yet paid, calmly walked out of the store in it while his unsuspecting saleslady was hunting up a few more coats that the villain had expressed a desire to see. What a furor that created and how important our little detective Johnnie acted when he traced the man and triumphantly brought the coat back. His only regret was that the thief himself jumped out of a window and escaped at the very moment when he was being arrested. Poor Johnnie, that must have been the big moment of his rather un-eventful life, for usually he spent his days wandering aimlessly around the store with his hat on his head, firmly convinced that thus disguised he would deceive customers with shop-lifting tendencies and make them think that he was a customer himself. Round and round the store he'd shuffle, suspiciously eyeing all the honest customers and yawning desperately, until finally he'd fall asleep in one of the fur closets, to the relief of the shop lifters.

But the greatest excitement of all came one day when my Navy Man unexpectedly appeared in the fur de-partment and in a perfectly audible voice—heard by nearly all the sales force idly grouped together (as it happened to be a morning when there were no cus-tomers), asked me whether we were going to be mar-ried that day. Whereupon Mr. Makepeace hearing that astounding question, most considerately let me have the afternoon off and I departed to the accompaniment of a chorus of congratulations from my fellow workers. The next morning seeing me as I came into the store, they were quite disappointed, having decided that I was to be married the previous day and that they would never lay eyes on me again. The young girls even ran out from behind the counter, where they sold furs by the yard, and surrounded me demanding excitedly:

"Oh! Irina, why didn't you marry your Rabbit? . . .

your Squirrel? . . . your Kangaroo? . . ." meaning my Navy Man, of course, for, as we thought all day long about nothing but furs, we had reached the point where we naturally called human beings by the names of various animals.

On the whole I liked the fur department better than any other place in which I had worked and it was quite a shock to me, when, one day, Mr. Makepeace gravely announced to the assembled sales force that, as the fur season was practically over, he would have to cut down his staff, keeping only those that had been with him a long time and transferring us, the newcomers, to other departments. And it was with real regret that a week later I bade my fur companions good-by and moved downstairs to my new quarters, the picture galleries. Consisting of three small rooms and one larger one, these galleries had no windows and consequently were always lighted by electricity, so that during the three following months I never saw daylight except early in the morning. That unnatural condition soon affected my eyes and made me suffer a good deal, until I took to wearing glasses whenever I read. Then too, owing to the absence of windows, the ventilation in the galleries was atrocious and from the stale air and the dust I developed a nasty, dry cough that lasted all the while that I worked there.

My new boss, an effeminate-looking man of about

forty-five, with unnaturally wide, womanish hips, which he swayed suggestively every time he moved, was a querulous, hysterical, capricious individual with whom I did not get on at all. But my two other companions were decidedly nice: Mrs. Luke, comfortable, worldly wise, tactful and soothing, and poor old Mr. Dixie, moth-eaten and pathetic who firmly believed that yeast tablets would stop the progress of the frightful disease that was slowly but surely bringing him to his grave.

Besides selling the pictures that hung on the walls and were stacked in corners on the floor, we had several special exhibits in our galleries which attracted crowds of people and kept us very busy. It was during one of those sales that a florid-looking man bought an enormous picture from me (a terror that I was ashamed to sell him) and appeared so pleased with his purchase that he generously offered me a fifty-cent tip.

Then one afternoon just as I was having a bad spell of coughing, a young woman, by the name of Mrs. Judson, one of the queens of Metropole's élite, came into the picture gallery looking for me. Obsequiously my boss ran behind her swaying his hips more than ever in the excitement of having such a wealthy customer and in a shrill voice with many elegant gestures and significant raisings of his eyebrows told me to be sure to take good care of her. I had met her only once before and was much surprised when instead of asking to look at pictures she invited me to dinner next evening.

"I've heard a lot about you and I'd like to know you better," she said in answer to my look of surprise, and as I liked her at once I accepted her invitation.

But the following morning I woke up with a high fever and a cough so painfully shattering that I had to call up Mrs. Judson and tell her as best I could in a husky whisper, that I would not be able to dine with her that night. Then Lena, the hotel chambermaid, a roly-poly little German girl with pink cheeks, blue eyes, flaxen hair and the sweetest disposition in the world, who had taken a special liking to me ever since I arrived at the Sidewater Hotel, came bustling along in her starched blue frock and white cap and seeing me in such a deplorable condition threw up her hands exclaiming:

"Ach, du lieber Gott!" and started to do the best she could to help me. A warm bath, fresh bed linen, an extra blanket and a cup of hot tea was all she could think of, until hearing me cough she suddenly remembered a wonderful medicine that a friend of hers, another chambermaid on the same floor, was taking for her cough, and rushing out of the room returned in a few minutes with some nasty-looking stuff which she obliged me to swallow. But as the morning hours passed I grew worse and worse and could hardly raise my head or speak above a whisper, when about noon Mrs. Judson came in, carrying an armful of yellow roses, and radiant in a beautiful mink coat which I could not help appraising even though my professional "fur" eye was becoming somewhat dimmed.

"One mink coat," I thought approvingly, "two mink coats, three mink coats, four and five . . ." and then I saw hundreds and thousands of them dancing around me with real arms and legs in their rightful places but without any heads.

"Do you feel very ill?" asked Mrs. Judson, bending over me as I tried to push away those headless coats that were beginning to stifle me as they pressed closer and closer. With difficulty I opened my eyes.

"Why, no," I answered, trying hard not to cough and choking in the effort. "I'm all right, only a bad cold—that's all, but I'm afraid I won't be able to come to your party to-night."

"I'll call a doctor right away," she declared energetically, seating herself at the telephone and beginning to look up a number in the directory.

"Oh, no, no, please don't," I cried, much alarmed at the suggestion, as my finances were then painfully low, in fact I had only $122 in the bank, and that was all I possessed in the world. But she didn't pay any attention to my protest and in a decided voice called up the number she had been looking for. Then everything became dim and blurred for me once more and that condition must have lasted for a long while, as the next thing I remember when I opened my burning, aching eyes was the presence of a doctor in a white coat and of a trained nurse on either side of me, while at the foot of my bed stood Mrs. Judson, Lyta Barr and Lena, the little German maid. In those few minutes of lucidity I could hear the words: "pneumonia, crisis, night nurse," pronounced very softly and then Lena's shrill voice ringing out in anxiety: "Hermonia? Ach vie schrecklich! Oh, vot iss dat—hermonia?" followed by Lyta Barr's quick whisper: "Hush, Lena, not hermonia but pneumonia, don't you understand?"

And then again unconsciousness and strange mysterious wanderings in the twilight of the great valley of death. When at last the crisis had passed and I was pronounced out of danger—I felt so weak, so utterly exhausted that all I could do was to lie very quietly without saying a word for hours at a time. It seemed to me that only then I understood how dreadfully tired I was, with a fatigue that had grown on me little by little, ever since the day when my train pulled out of the Petrograd Baltic station, carrying me into exile. First the War, then the Revolution, then Exile—what years they had been! Years of anxiety, sorrow, hunger, poverty, sickness and hard work and with barely any rest in between. Oh, I was so tired, so desperately tired!

But because I was still young and full of tremendous vitality, a vitality that nothing seemed able to destroy, I slept on and on and during that sleep a new life seemed to flow through my veins. Gradually I began to recover. Then, when I was able to sit up in my bed and look around me, I realized that everything had been done by Mrs. Judson to help me pull through and make me comfortable. Doctor, nurses, medicine, the right kind of food, wine, beautiful yellow roses in tall glasses on all my tables, silk night-gowns, a warm quilted bed jacket, a lace cap, a white velvet coverlet, a golden colored silk robe lined with pink satin, slippers of gold brocade, lovely old china cups and saucers, and fragile crystal tumblers out of which I drank my medicine—hundreds of dollars had been spent on me by some one who hardly knew me, some one who out of purest charity had undoubtedly saved my life and brought beauty into it. And then as a climax to it all came the day when she, who had done all this for me, offered to buy the one really valuable thing I possessed and that Dr. Golder had brought out of Russia for me: my lace Court dress, which had once belonged to my great grandmother, Princess Elizabeth Paskevitch of Warsaw, in the days when she was Vicereine of Poland. My mother had given it to me at the time of my marriage to Count Alexander Keller, on the same day that she gave me the diamond necklace and told me then not to forget that that lace Court dress was as valuable as the diamonds. I often thought of her words when I wore it at Court functions, the very last time being at the great reception at the Winter Palace in honor of the Romanoff tercentenary, when the Empress was much amused because, as I had just bobbed my hair, my pearl and diamond head dress, the "kokoshnik," wouldn't keep straight on my head. Then all through the Revolution the dress hung unmolested in my closet at the hospital, together with my Red Cross uniforms and aprons, for the soldiers and their women who searched our rooms over and over again, never realized the value of lace and never paid the slightest attention to that dress. Finally when I left Russia it remained in the keeping of my faithful old maid who later on sent it to me through Dr. Golder. And I cannot describe my amazement when on opening the little trunk which he had brought me all the way from Russia to London, I beheld on top of everything else my famous lace Court dress. It seemed so strange, so incongruous to see it in that humble little room of mine and then to remember my mother's words that it was as valuable as the diamond necklace. I tried to sell it in London but was unsuccessful, for times were hard then and neither Christie nor Duveen could dispose of it for the price which they considered fair. Then I brought it to America in one of the two little suitcases that crossed the ocean with me and that carried all my worldly goods. After that the dress hung in the closet of the dingy boarding house in Dawn, and in my tiny apartment in Grasshopper Street,—and in the Sidewater hotel, until the day when Mrs. Judson saw it and immediately offered to buy it.

"It is one of the most beautiful things I have ever seen and I'll have it appraised by the Museum," she said, taking it away with her and then returned two days later saying that they had estimated it at seven thousand dollars and that she had brought me a check for that sum as she loved rare old lace, collected it, and was anxious to add my dress to her collection.

"Seven thousand dollars does not mean much to me, for really I have a disgusting lot of money," she said laughingly when I timidly asked her whether she could really afford to part with such an enormous sum. "But it might be of some use to you," she continued, while breathlessly I stared at her, my heart thumping so hard that it hurt.

"Be of use to me?" I whispered, nearly crying from excitement, "why, it means rest, comfort, ease, riches . . . and even more than that . . ." I added to myself. Yes, more than all that, for with seven thousand dollars belonging to me I was no longer the penniless exile who did not dare marry the man she wanted, because she was ashamed of being so poor, ashamed of not being able to buy herself the humblest trousseau, ashamed to think she would have to depend on him for every penny she needed. Now I felt independent, secure, rich, and though I could not remove the other obstacles of which the worst was the fact that I had had such a tragic past, still I realized that if he wanted me "just as I was," battered and bruised and hurt all over, he was the best judge, for after all he was not a boy but a mature and experienced man.

And so one evening seated by my open window, overlooking the shining water below, I wrote my Navy Man a long letter and asked him to come to me at once. A few days later he arrived and as we paced up and down my favorite walk in the quiet gardens of the hotel by the lake, we came to the final decision that we were going to be married very soon.

"Why not to-day?" he inquired briskly, but I obstinately shook my head, saying that things had to be done right, that I couldn't possibly be married in my old jersey working dress and that I had to get a small trousseau.

"Don't be silly, you could buy a new frock in ten minutes," he argued. But I wouldn't give in.

"It isn't only the question of a new frock, it's lots of other things that a man knows nothing about," I said firmly, and finally he agreed.

I was disappointed to see that he did not share my enthusiasm about my newly acquired fortune, but actually seemed to regret that I was not coming to him penniless in the shabby old jersey working frock.

"It's all right, you may keep the money and do whatever you like with it, but don't mention it again, it's yours and doesn't concern me at all," he said quite rudely, I thought, and so, tactfully, I changed the conversation.

We decided that he'd come back in two weeks and that we would get married then. But as I went with him to the station that evening to see him off, I suddenly began to cry. I was still rather shaky and hated to part with him again.

"So that's the way you feel?" he inquired, staring at me thoughtfully and softly whistling to himself. "All right, come on, we'll find a judge and a preacher," he shouted, firmly grasping me by my arm and making me run from the train shed through the station, and into a taxi.

"But not in this dress!" I cried weakly.

"Oh, yes, in that dress. . . ."

And three hours later we were married!

"Congratulations, little Russky, you're an American now," he said, after we had been pronounced man and wife, "and remember you belong to the present and the future, for your old world did end, the interlude in exile is over and now your life in a new world begins."